THE SLEEPY INLET

Memories of Life on Little Bulls Island

Mary Magwood Causey

Copyright © 2014 Mary Magwood Causey
All rights reserved.

ISBN: 1500991686
ISBN 13: 9781500991685
Library of Congress Control Number: 2014915731
CreateSpace Independent Publishing Platform,
North Charleston, South Carolina

This book is dedicated to the memory of my earthly parents, Clarence and Ethel Magwood, for true wealth in the treasured memories they gave me on this earth and to my heavenly Father, who gives me wealth and joy in eternal life both now and forever.

Mary Magwood Causey

CONTENTS

	PROLOGUE	IX
1.	OUR HOME	1
2.	LITTLE BULLS ISLAND	8
3.	ALMOST A DOZEN	27
4.	PLAYFUL LIVING	38
5.	SETTING THE SEINE	48
6.	MARSH-HENNING AND FIDDLERING	50
7.	OLD JOE	53
8.	THE LIVELIHOOD	56
9.	OLD-FASHIONED REMEDIES	61
10.	TALL TALES	69
	THE PLAT-EYE	69
	TIGER BILL	72
11.	TRIPS TO THE MAINLAND	75
12.	HOLIDAYS	78
13.	ISLAND DREAMS	82
14.	DIRECTIONS FOR A ROLEY-POLEY	85
15.	CHANGED FOR LIFE	95
16.	EPILOGUE: WHAT IS BEAUTY?	107

17.	SOME OF MY OWN FAVORITE RECIPES	114
18.	ACKNOWLEDGMENTS	125
19.	INDEX OF POEMS	126
20.	ABOUT THE AUTHOR	128

"THE ISLAND"

Surrounded by the smells and
Swells of marsh and beach
Lies Little Bulls Island
And the house built from
Shipwrecked timbers, resting
On creosote posts, with the
Screened-in porch where I
Shared Poppa's knee
With his banjo.
And I can still feel
Oyster shells crushed beneath
Bare feet as I walked to
The dock at night watching
Channel markers lighting
The path to the city.
And I remember *The Squeaking
Door* and *Gunsmoke* on
The radio while playing Old
Maid by a kerosene light.
And I feel the emptiness
Like the inlet after the
Yachts went away, and the
Freight from palmettos cracking
And chickens thumping under
The house at night. And I
Can still see Poppa's eyes
When I called his dream
A prison.

PROLOGUE

At around age fifteen, when all of my friends were dating, doing the shag, and frolicking at the beach, I began to resent going to the island. I, too, wanted to be a part of the dating scene. I told Poppa that his beloved island was like a prison, and his eyes mirrored the hurt of my words. At that stage of our lives Momma wanted to live at Little Bulls with Poppa year-round because I was the last one in school, so I was sent to live with my sister and her husband in Mount Pleasant. After this point, trips to the island were rare, and I did not return for a long stay until after I was married. How differently we see things when we grow older. It is only after we lose the once-simple pleasures of our lives that we can truly appreciate them. After work, raising a family, and the rat race of material gain pulled me into the vice of time constraints, I longed to have the serenity and beauty of the island once more. It was then that I understood the joy Poppa cherished in being separated from the stress of life; the uniqueness of a world with no phones, no communication from the outside-just the beauty and haunting peacefulness of the sleepy inlet.

MARY MAGWOOD CAUSEY

"PRISONER OF THE SEA"

I set sail upon the sea,
My heart and soul to soar.
To leave my troubles far behind
And think of them no more.

To taste the salt mist on my lips,
To feel the caress of an ocean breeze.
While traveling waves of azure blue
That fold to jade and emerald seas.

Like the wind beneath a new bird,
I rise on peaks of white,
That fade to gentle ripples
Echoing secrets of the night.

With the clouds as my only cover,
And the darkness my endless foe,
I plunge above the deepness
With its mysteries locked below.

As each day dawns a new start,
My spirit again set free,
I travel on life's path my way
In love and bondage with the sea.

THE SLEEPY INLET

"SHRIMP BOATS ARE COMING IN"

The inlet sleeps peacefully until the tide starts in
Bringing shrimp boats round the bend.
Tall masts sway, rolling side to side, from the motion
Of the wind. Shrimp boats are coming in.

Sea gulls dive for trash raked from the catch
Of shrimp, crab, and fish, tangled in the nets.
Bronzed hands, reddened from the prick of
Snapping shrimp heads two at a time,
Separate the trash from treasure.

Within her belly, crates of ice
Protect the vessel's haul bound for
Restaurants like Ronnie's or RB's.
Shrimp boats are coming in.

A jealous mistress is the sea,
And work lasts from dusk to dawn.
Prepare the deck and cast the lines;
Pass a warm cup of ease to take
The chill out of the day.
Shrimp boats are coming in.

MARY MAGWOOD CAUSEY

"THE SANDBAR"

The endless sea calls to me;
Its pounding surf like broken glass.
As it rolls in and out the inlet,
My boat glides through the narrow pass.

Carefully, for sandbars hide
To trap their careless prey
And strand them on the hidden bar
So they cannot get away.

No mercy has the angry sea
Its depths reveal the score
Of those who fought it fearlessly
Then washed upon the shore.

Hold back your trashing water
For one who trusts you so;
Give this captain a little grace
As you rise to let him go.

One degree starboard
Aim the stern towards the shore
And I will bid you farewell
As I am crossing ocean's floor.

OUR HOME

A cool mist touched my face as I ran down the path to the dock, excited about the boats making their way through the narrow strait of the inlet. Shrimp boats did not come in often, because the sandbar was treacherous, changing its shape almost weekly as the silt and sand washed from bar to beach and back again. A captain had to know the inlet well to manage the pass without beaching his boat, something my brothers had managed to perfect through the years. Poppa had witnessed many a boat breaking apart because the captain made a mistake in judgment while maneuvering the course. Often, a captain would have to wait for the incoming tide to lift the boat from the sand before continuing into the inlet.

In fact, the house where we lived at Price's Inlet had been built by my poppa using the materials from ships wrecked along Capers and Bulls Beaches. Through the years, the house, marked by old beams, low ceilings, and narrow door openings, had weathered many a storm. Sadly, the house was finally destroyed after Hurricane Hugo with only the creosote pilings and steps remaining. The house, along with the many bateaux he built, affirmed Poppa's skill as a carpenter. I can still smell the creosote from the tar on the tin where he would patch a leak or add another coat to preserve the pilings under the house.

The main house was divided into two parts by a central sunken entrance with exterior doors at each end. On one side was a large kitchen with an old table in the center covered with a red-checkered plastic tablecloth . An antique bureau held the few dishes Momma treasured, and hidden among those was Poppa's jar of "rock and rye." In the corner of the room was a built-in pantry where all the dry goods were stored for daily use in the kitchen. A screened porch located off the kitchen held the table where most summer meals were eaten. The sweet smell of the large old salt water cedars blooming with their soft pink flowers, as well as the chirping from the colorful parakeets that were once native to this area, added a special flair to our mealtime. As the central location for many family activities, the porch was where we listened to Poppa's foot-tapping tunes on the banjo, and it was where Poppa spent time napping in a rocker or resting as he was shaved. There were three bedrooms: Momma and Poppa's, a small bedroom between the living room and their room, where I slept, and another bedroom on the opposite side, fondly known as the "Little Room." Located just off Momma and Poppa's room was the bathroom area, which contained the "potty bucket," and in much later days a real bathtub. Of course, there was never running water to the tub. Water had to be carried in from the outside cistern, heated on the wooden stove, and then bucketed to fill the tub.

The attic area was divided into two bedrooms, and Lilly used one of these as her room, though she spent most nights sleeping in the living room chair. Momma and Poppa's bedroom and the Little Room had wood-burning fireplaces, the only means of heat in the house. A small can of kerosene was always handy to start the fire on cold winter nights. There was no electricity, running water, or indoor plumbing, just a generator that Poppa would crank up on really special occasions, otherwise, we read and worked

by kerosene lamps. All of the water used for cooking or bathing was obtained from a gutter system that spilled into two cisterns. One cistern held drinking water, and the other held water used for miscellaneous tasks such as washing dishes or bathing. Two large pails were filled daily and brought to the kitchen for these purposes. When there was a dry spell, providing little water to fill the cisterns, we went to Big Bulls Beach and pumped water from the well Poppa had dug there, then hauled it back to the island in wash tubs. At one time, Poppa's family owned Big Bulls, and later Poppa owned a small part, but he sold it back to the government. At bath time, water had to be boiled on the wood stove then a washtub was filled with the hot water, and cold water was added to the desired temperature. One of the large tubs Momma used for washing clothes doubled as a bathtub. Because of the hassle and the frequent scarcity of water, a full bath was not taken but once, or maybe twice, a week. At nighttime, the toilet was a bucket that was kept inside the house in the bathroom area, and it had to be emptied at the outhouse the next morning. This was one chore I particularly hated, and I always managed to talk my sister

Lilly into doing it for me. Using the outhouse during the daytime was bad enough, but no one liked to venture there at night. The outhouse had two sides, one for men and one for the ladies, and it was smart to check the inside of the hole before preparing to seat oneself. Once when I did this, a large snake was peering up at me; after that, I never wanted to use the outhouse again. On many occasions, one of us would find ourselves at the outhouse without toilet tissue. This was one thing that developed our family's talent for loud yelling voices. A person had to be able to shout loud enough for someone at the house to hear them, and hope they would be available to provide the much needed roll of tissue. This also helped to develop patience because sometimes you waited as much as thirty minutes. Making a trip to the outhouse at night was not a task one took lightly. It was often cold or much too hot, and there could be any number of creatures lurking in wait.

Momma did all the family laundry on an old-timey scrubboard and washtub. First, a fire was built out by the wash shed to get the water hot enough to scald the germs from the clothes. The scrub pot was set on top of four irons protruding from the ground, and a wood fire was built in the pit beneath. Next Momma had to haul water to the wash shed, where she dowsed the clothes up and down the scrub board with a healthy dose of Octagon soap. A separate tub of clean, cold water was used for rinsing, and then the clothes were hand wrung and set in another tub to be hung on the line to dry. It takes real skill to use a scrubboard and not scrape all the skin off one's knuckles. Momma did not entrust this task to us girls, but we did have the job of hanging them out and bringing in the laundry to be folded. The boys often helped build the fire or haul the water to the tubs. On stormy summer afternoons, we had to hustle to retrieve the clothes before they were soaked, requiring them to possibly need rewashing.

Poppa and Momma did grocery shopping in large quantity, buying cases of items like corned beef, Vienna sausage, Spam, etc.

from a wholesale company downtown. These items were stored in the generator house. Milk and perishable commodities were bought on the periodic trips to the mainland when fish were taken to market. There was always a large string of bananas hanging at the dock, because Poppa was friends with someone at the waterfront who kept us supplied. Perishables were stored in the icehouse until Poppa broke down at Momma's pleading and put in a propane gas refrigerator. The gas-powered refrigerator was a tremendously delightful appliance, making daily trips to the dock unnecessary, but it was also a source of argument. Momma forbade anyone to open the door unless she so instructed, and although Lilly often sneaked in for treats, she always fussed and told on us for doing so. Later, a gas stove was added, but Momma always preferred cooking on the old wood stove. There was always a large container of lard atop the stove. Poppa or the boys typically chopped the wood for the stove and fireplace heat, and the girls had to bring a load into the house each day. After the older boys were gone, we girls had our turn at wood chopping, too. Actually, I thought it was fun, but I didn't relish the kidding I took in high school over the large muscles it developed in my upper arms. A wood box was stored just behind the wood stove. The old house managed to make it through many a storm such as Gracie and David, but Hurricane Hugo took its toll, leaving nothing but the concrete steps and creosote posts as a monument to our heritage. I'm glad that Poppa was not alive for Hugo, because even when a major storm was predicted, he would not leave the island. During one fierce storm, everyone stayed on the island, and the water became so high in the yard, that my brother Junior gave all my siblings rides in his canoe made from an old airplane wing found on the beach. At times, the unusually high marsh-hen tides brought the water into our yard, so we became shrimp boat captains, racing the wooden sailboats Poppa had made us through the salty waters. Usually, when a category two or higher storm was predicted, Poppa sent us all to the mainland for safety. He remained at the island securing all the boats, getting the chickens cooped in the pen, and making sure the pigs were safe. Once when we returned from a bad storm, Sukie, the only pig left, was standing on the back porch of the house.

THE SLEEPY INLET

"JUNIOR-THE CAPTAIN"

Red of eye and red of face,
Weathered by the sea's embrace,
You wear a cap to show your fate;
A vessel captain and I, your mate.

With a voice as rough as the raging sea,
Flavored by salt mist running free,
Words not spoken by the polished few,
Have become an integral part of you.

And tales you spin with an artist's care,
Make us feel as if we were there—
Riding across the sea caps white,
Hauling the nets with shoreline in sight.

Though you walk with a limp instead of a spark,
And it's getting harder to see in the dark,
Your lifelong work can't be laid aside,
So you wait and watch for the outgoing tide.

Your boat made ready, the doors set in place,
You head for the sea, asking God's grace.
For though you do well hiding it from view,
There is a softer, gentler side of you.

And as the sun reaches down to kiss the sea,
The clouds unfold around you and me.
You become as one with the world you know
Hand-in-hand with God, your nets in tow.

LITTLE BULLS ISLAND

Located a bit northeast and approximately fifteen miles by water from Mount Pleasant, Little Bulls Island is nestled diagonally across from Big Bulls and directly behind Capers Beach in Price's Inlet. If you are traveling down the inland waterway from Charleston, take a right at buoy 86 and then follow the creek to the inlet. Little Bulls is only about three to four acres of highland surrounded by marsh. Poppa, Junior, and my brothers built a dike down the quarter-acre path to the dock, which was covered entirely in oyster shells, on which we learned to travel with hardened bare feet. We never wore shoes unless we were in school. Hip boots were the only other footwear needed at the island, and those were for gathering oysters, clams, or shrimp and fish. There was a small beach that we called "Little Beach" attached to the Capers side of the island. There were two or three little oyster banks that dotted the perimeter of the beach. At outgoing tide, we could almost walk across the creek between Little Beach and Capers. Over the years, erosion made Little Beach more a part of Caper's than our island.

Poppa and Junior built a shell dike path down to the Little Beach area and to the dock at Schooner Creek, which was and still is a favorite spot for sheepshead fishing. There was an area further up the creek that Poppa staked off, known as the "sheepshead racks" where sheepshead were typically very plentiful and many fishermen went to make a large haul. A brackish pond was dug not far from the house with a large dike surrounding it, and this was stocked with ducks. A spillway out-flowed to the marsh in order to regulate the height of the water in the pond. The wash shed was located near the house end of the pond with the chicken coop and outhouse at the far right end. There were four houses located on the island, the main house where we lived (which shrank as I got older); a small white house built by my half-sister Viola and her husband, Willie Duck, a toolshed that once housed Old Bill, a black man that worked for Poppa for many years and helped Momma take care of us children; and a cabin with two rooms that Poppa rented out to yachtsmen for weekend stays. My brothers, Bucky and Jimmy, used one side of the cabin as their sleeping quarters when it was not rented.

When a boat narrowed the bend, making the markings on the side visible, more often than not it was the trawler, The Skipper and Wayne, which belonged to our brother Junior. He was known by all of us as Junior to make the distinction between him and Poppa. Most everyone called Poppa Captain Clarence, a title later inherited by Junior. Whenever Junior or anyone stopped at the dock for a visit, Momma always cooked a feast. She would light up the wood stove in the kitchen, and put on a pot of grits. She would get some fresh shrimp from the boat to make shrimp with brown gravy and grits, one of Poppa's favorites. Our family was eating that as a poor man's dish long before it became a gourmet entree at most local restaurants. Grits (and usually fish) was a daily part of our diet. Poppa rose before Momma each morning and started the grits and coffee, and then Momma would finish making the breakfast when she got up. Sometimes boats would stop by our dock for a good meal and a short rest before taking their haul to market along the Intra-coastal Waterway channel. Momma always offered to share whatever we had to eat; hospitality was definitely one of Momma's spiritual gifts.

Whenever a shrimp boat came into the inlet, the seagulls were always close behind to feed off the scraps of unusable fish. If we were lucky, there would be extra flounder Poppa could clean for supper. Although fish was a frequent part of our diet, I hated all fish except flounder, and it was a treat not to have mullet or mullet roe to eat with the grits, even though this is still one of my brother Andrew's favorites. Because Momma had lived through the depression, a fact of which we were often reminded, she was especially conservative and stern about us eating what was put before us. I was stubborn, too, and once I sat in front of a bowl of okra soup for two hours before she finally let me get up to do the dishes. Poppa, on the other hand, was totally laid back about our eating habits, and would always say, "Ethel, leave Mame (Poppa had nicknames for each of us) alone now." Poppa could be sweet-talked into just about anything by us girls, for he loved us so very much. Poppa had loads of favorite dishes, and Momma delighted in making them for him. I still get queasy just thinking about the bulging eyes staring up from his favorite fish head stew. We raised pigs on the island as well as chickens, and once we even had a lamb that had wandered from Capers Beach. A slop bucket was kept in the kitchen under the meat grinder to catch all scraps that would later provide a feast for the pigs. We each had our turn at slopping the pigs after supper each night. I don't remember exactly why or when we stopped raising pigs, but I suppose it got to be too much work for Poppa.

Watching Poppa and Momma slaughter the pigs or chickens for food was an occasion we did not relish. This was because we knew the pending task of cleaning up the debris from the slaughter would be assigned to us. We always managed to make a friend of one of the pigs, such as "Sukie," so we could not bear to watch as they met their ultimate fate. The uncured smell of fresh pork cooking resembles a strong, cheap perfume, so I was never able to make myself eat it. Momma did not waste any part of the pig, either. She made cracklings from the skin and hog's head cheese with the head. Poppa loved the hog's head cheese. The dish resembled a loaf type product like liver pudding.

FISH CHOWDER

Fry 5–6 strips of bacon
Add 1 large onion diced
2 stalks of celery diced
4 fresh tomatoes diced (or 1 can)
6–8 flounder filets skinned
6–8 Sheepshead filets skinned
6 potatoes diced
Salt, pepper, garlic to taste
1–2 teaspoons Tabasco (to desired temperature)
2 tablespoons Worcestershire sauce
4 quarts water
Cook all in large pot until and taste test till all done

(Secret recipe of my brother Dan Magwood)

One of Momma's greatest skills, though, was baking, and our home was always filled with the aroma of yeast biscuits and rolls, donuts, cakes, or divinity fudge. She made one of the best cherry nut cakes at Christmastime, and I have loved keeping the tradition of making it each year.

POOR MAN'S STEW

Brown 1 chopped onion in a teaspoon of olive oil, in a large pot
Add 2 tablespoons flour
Add 2 cans of corned beef
Add 2 quarts water
Add 4–5 diced potatoes
Add 2 carrots diced round
Salt and pepper to taste
Touch of Worcestershire Sauce
Cook on medium heat until all vegetables tender
Thicken to light consistency
Eat over rice
(This was a dish we had often—I hated it!)

MARY MAGWOOD CAUSEY

SHRIMP & BROWN GRAVY

Fry 3–4 strips of bacon in a pan
Brown with 1/2 cup chopped onion
Add 1–2 tablespoons flour to brown
Add about 1 cup water to thin
Add 1 lb. peeled and deveined shrimp
Add 1/2 cup of half-and-half
(Add mushrooms if desired)
Salt and pepper to taste
Touch of garlic
Cook on low till dish reaches consistency desired
Eat over grits

(Once a poor man's dish)

THE SLEEPY INLET

OLD-FASHIONED CORN PIE

3 cans creamed corn
Beat in 3 eggs, one at a time
Add 3/4–1 cup sugar (can substitute artificial sweetener)
2 tablespoons vanilla
2 tablespoons flour
1 can evaporated milk (or use skim milk)
Mix all in large casserole dish
Place casserole dish in pan of water
Bake in 300-degree oven for about 1 1/2 hours
Until the dish thickens well
(Momma made this often, and it is still one of my favorites)

SHRIMP CREOLE

1 large chopped onion
4–5 strips diced bacon
2 medium diced bell peppers
1 cup diced sausage (if desired)
2 lb. peeled and deveined shrimp
1–2 teaspoons Tabasco, as desired
2–3 tablespoons Worcestershire sauce
1 large can of tomato paste
2 medium cans tomato sauce
5–6 cans water
2–3 tablespoons flour
1 teaspoon sugar
Salt and pepper to taste
1 teaspoon celery salt

Brown onion, bacon, bell pepper, sausage, and flour. Add tomato paste, tomato sauce, water, and seasonings. Cook on medium about 2 hours. Add shrimp and cook 15 to 20 minutes until shrimp are done.

Eat over rice

EASY CLAM CHOWDER

1 can cream of celery soup
1 can cream of mushroom soup
1/2-pint ground clams with juice
Salt and pepper to taste
Hint of garlic
2 cans water

Cook on medium heat until smooth

During the day, the chickens were let out of their pen into the house yard, where we fed them chicken scratch. Each day we gathered the brown eggs for cooking. Sometimes if a hen sat too long on the eggs, when the egg was broken, a bloody streak appeared, which indicated a chick embryo inside. This is one reason many of us cannot eat fresh eggs today, although their rich yolk makes them ideal for baking purposes. The chickens often laid eggs all around the grounds surrounding the house and pond, so we made a game of finding the nest. Whenever chicken was on the menu, Momma picked the fattest hen, took it to the wood block, and chopped its head off. The body of the chicken continued to jerk about like a frightened cat. Once the headless form settled down, we washed and picked the chicken clean, then Momma cut it up for frying or perhaps for a chicken and dumpling (today when I purchase chicken, it is always precut). At night if we did not get all the chickens in the coop, they would nest under the house, thumping all through the night. Their thumping sound, along with the rustling of the palms in the summer breeze, provided a haunting sound that would have frightened almost anyone. It kept me from sleeping many lonely summer nights.

   Poppa loved to antagonize the roosters who strolled proudly around the yard. He picked at one of the roosters until the rooster would fly at him, pecking away. I have heard of cockfighting, but I always thought it required two roosters. When Poppa tired of his folly, he would catch the rooster and rock him to sleep by tucking his head under his wing, and he taught us to do this with the chickens as well. It was almost like hypnosis, because they only slept for a few minutes and then got up dazed. Momma did not like Poppa picking at the rooster, nor did we, because it made the rooster mean, and then we feared walking around the yard because he would peck us without provocation.

   While Momma loved Poppa very much, her German temper often flared with little reason. When she was angry with Poppa, we could hear her hollering for him as far as Bulls Beach. She stood at the back of Little Creek and "whooped" when dinner was ready. Momma did not like to be kept waiting, especially when she came in from a day of gathering oysters and had to prepare a hot meal. Her tasks as a parent, additional breadwinner, and housekeeper were never really done. Momma loved each of us in her own way, but showing love was harder for her than receiving love. I never met her mother who was of full German descent because she died of tuberculosis when Momma was about eight. She was raised by an unloving stepmother, so it is easy to understand why she needed love so deeply. My maternal grandfather was French, and had the appearance of a rough sea captain. He always had his favorite pipe tucked in the corner of his mouth. I can't say I ever remember him saying anything loving to me at all.

Momma was given the final decision regarding us children, so we all had annual trips to the dentist and to the doctor for our shots. Poppa saw no value in material things, nor much need of doctors, and really did not care much about whether or not we had new clothes or shoes to wear. Momma, however, made sure that every Easter and at the beginning of school, we had a new dress and new shoes.

Momma never seemed to stop working. Even when she settled down at day's end, she was crocheting blankets, bedspreads, or scarves for someone. Each time one of us had a baby, she crocheted a baby afghan in our favorite color. Since we had no heat except the fireplace, Momma made patchwork quilts for each bed. Though she didn't crochet clothes as a general rule, I recall that when I was in the first grade, Momma made me a red-and-white crocheted dress, which I thought was really special. The kids at school made fun of me, though, and I didn't understand why. Later, I realized it was because they considered us "poor" people, and they thought we could not afford to buy clothes. The love that Momma put into her work seemed to flow through to the wearer. I wish I had her skill, but all I can do is a simple popcorn stitch. My sister Tommie inherited Momma's skill with the needle, but Earl could do some fancy loop rugs, too. Other than crocheting, Momma loved to read magazines, and she always had a large supply of *McCall's* or *Ladies' Home Journal* as well as *True Romance*. Reading her Bible was usually the last thing she did before falling asleep. My sister and I always looked forward to the discarded *McCall's* so we could cut out the Betsy McCall paper dolls, with which we loved to play. After a while, we had quite a supply of different attire for little "Miss Betsy," which was kept in an old cigar box (Momma worked at the cigar factory downtown in the early years of marriage). The cigar box traveled back and forth with us from Little Bulls to Sullivan's Island for many years.

Whenever Momma was in the baking mood, the kitchen was lined from table to stove with pans of various goods. We loved the homemade donuts she fried, and relished the chance to devour the holes. She did not waste one bit of the dough! Once the hot donuts were removed from the skillet, they were placed on paper to drain the grease, then dusted with sugar and cinnamon or powdered sugar. She had many other specialties, like homemade cinnamon rolls, fresh-baked yeast bread, and terrific corn bread. Baking is a joy for me as well, and when I am in the baking mode, there are never fewer than four or five items being made at one time. My sister Tommie enjoys baking and cooking about as well as I do. It is probably not much of a wonder, however, that many of us have high cholesterol, since lard was a staple in all of the baking. Another negative factor in all the sweets is that Momma, Lilly, Jr., Andrew, and Virgie developed type 2 diabetes.

Each summer, Momma went to the mountains with my sister-in-law, and around age twelve, I was considered old enough to accept some responsibility, so I was left to cook the meals for Poppa and Lilly. I had a wonderful recipe for peanut butter cookies, which Poppa really liked. He could eat four or five

cookies at one time without blinking. Even when the doctors said he should cut out sweets, he did not do so. He said, "I've eaten what I wanted all my life, and I'm not about to stop now." Since he lived to a ripe age of eighty-three without ever being hospitalized, perhaps his philosophy had some merit. Another favorite of Poppa's was corn beef hash mixed with ketchup then fried brown in an iron skillet.

One of the things we all learned, including the boys, was how to cook. The boys had to know how so they could take their turn cooking on the shrimp boats. Most of my brothers took pride in the fact that they could cook. Poppa had some favorite dishes he cooked, but the main job of preparing the meals was left to Momma. Poppa always griped, though, that she cooked way too much food for each meal. The variety was astounding: rice, beans, okra, pork chops, biscuits, and of course, pie or cake. Poppa's simple lifestyle required simple pleasures even when it came to food. He could survive on clabbered milk and toast.

All of my children learned to cook as well, and I am happy I passed this skill on to them. There are so many young women today who don't seem to know anything about cooking, and even more than that, they don't want to know. It seems there is a new trend for the man to participate more in the family food preparation. Maybe the old adage, "the way to a man's heart is through his stomach," is true after all.

THE SLEEPY INLET

"OUR MOTHER"

Hard work in life is what she knew,
The joys she felt were often few,
For she strived to give us more
Of the things she never had before.

Her hands worked like lightning,
As she cracked the oyster's shell.
I'd have to run to keep in step
As she hauled her goods to sell.

Our kitchen was always filled
With the aroma of a homemade good.
No one could make crab patties
Or yeast bread like my mother could.

Many children loved her greatly,
And these were not her own,
For she babysat with others
And gentle seeds of love were sown.

With eleven of us to raise,
Her tasks were never really done,
For even when she settled down,
She was crocheting memories for someone.

She gave each of us something special,
And we each know in our own hearts,
The sacrifices that she daily made
To give each of us life's start.

But I want to thank her most
For something precious she gave to me
Because in her almost dying once,
She set my spirit free.

If she had not suffered then,
I might not have known
How much Jesus loves each of us
And wants us for His own.

So, rest in peace now, mother;
Though we suffer at your loss,
I know we'll meet again one day
At that Old Rugged Cross.

"POPPA'S PEACE"

Salt marsh sprays his weathered face
As he steers his bateau to the beach
With Bucky beside him there.
Tide is full and time is short
To stake the gully's mouth
And capture there his prey.
Rocks weight the seine tight to the
Ocean's floor so no prize eludes him.
Delighting in his play, Captain Clarence
Casts his net to test the ocean's bounty.
Mullet leap into the air, gills taunt and
Scales gleaming, red beneath the sun.
Gravity draws the water slowly out
Calling sea creatures back into the deep.
Able to see in the shallow, the Captain
Spears a flounder from its bed,
No thought for the weakness of his heart.
He tugs the net to haul the fish ashore.
Then like a fish out of water, he
Grasps his pounding chest and
Falls into the gentle rippling water.
As waves caress, his body weakens,
And taking one final glance at Prices,
His eyes close for he is at peace
Beneath the sun, sand, and sea of life.

"FOR LILLY"

Lovely Rose of Sharon,
A rose is added to your bough,
A gentle, childlike spirit,
We were blessed awhile to know.

In love, God gave you to us,
And in love, He called you home.
Now your gentle, childlike spirit
Will no longer have to roam.

You'll rest among the angels
Where He prepared for you a place.
For Christ paved your way at Calvary
When He saved you by His grace.

So keep charge of special memories
Of times and joys we hold dear,
Until the bridegroom lights a candle
To bid each one of us draw near.

ALMOST A DOZEN

Junior was the oldest of my six brothers, and he was twenty years my senior. In fact, he was married before I was born. All of my brothers grew up on the sea, and a love for the sweet salt mist has followed them all their lives, each choosing to make his living from the sea. When the pluff mud marshes and gentle ocean breeze are in your blood, it is there for life, and you are truly free only in the peace you find in the wide open blue. Often, people mistook Junior for my father, something that made Poppa really angry. Poppa was sixty when I was born, and his appearance resembled that of a weathered fisherman, with soft gray eyes lined with red, accenting his tanned and wrinkled face. He had a small quarter saucer of gray hair at the base of his bald head and not one tooth in his mouth, which never stopped him from eating anything he wanted. In fact, one of his favorite things was a "Sugar Daddy" which he would suck until it was gone. You could spot him anywhere in his red-and-black checked flannel shirt, suspenders, and short cutoff pants—or dungarees in the winter. In the summertime, he was often dressed in only a pair of pants and suspenders with a pair of oyster boots on his feet. Dress was one of the most unimportant things on his agenda, and he never bought anything new because he was given all the necessary items for each special occasion such as his birthday or Christmas. Poppa always smelled of old spice and the sea and loved to eat crystallized ginger as a snack, a delight I also find quite enjoyable. Ginger is settling to the stomach. As long as I can remember, Poppa never shaved himself. He loved to have a shave at the barbershop in Mount Pleasant, but on the island, Momma had the chore of shaving him with an old-fashioned straight razor. He always complained that she was much too rough, and he feared she would slit his throat. Each of us girls had our chance at the task of shaving Poppa. I begged for the opportunity to show my skill with the razor, and finally he allowed me the privilege. I would soak his weathered face with a hot towel, lather the brush up in the mug, and dab his face lavishly with the soap (we didn't have canned shaving cream) Then I'd gently shave each side and lastly, his neck. More than the shaving, I enjoyed the conversations with Poppa during this time. Poppa was not one to get in a hurry about much, but when he worked, he worked hard. He was in bed before the chickens, up before the rooster, and napping after his lunch meal each day.

There were eleven of us in all, thirteen counting my two half-sisters, who were married by the time I was born. One of my half-sisters was the same age as my mother, and the other was a couple of years older. My sister Bernie Hills and her husband used to be the caretakers of Big Bulls, and she would bake Poppa cakes, and come to the far end of the beach and holler for Poppa to come and pick them up. My sister Viola never had children of her own, but loved to take us to her home in Florence for a summer stay. Once I asked my momma why she and Poppa had so many children, and she said "I was only eighteen when I got married, and no one talked about sex or anything back then." I replied, "Yes, but it seems like you would have caught on after a while." Of the eleven, there were—six boys and five girls—in my immediate family, and

THE SLEEPY INLET

although the ages were only one or two years apart as an average, we were not all at home at once. Thomasine, Earl, Andrew, and I were the ones going to school together, but Andrew left school early to help Poppa on the island. He worked with Poppa until he was drafted, and when he returned he got into the shrimping business with Poppa's help.

Poppa's first wife died after their third child was born. They lived on Big Bulls Island at the time, and she got really sick after the baby was born. Poppa went to the mainland to get a doctor (a trip then of several days), but his wife died before his return. The baby only lived for about a week. They are buried on Big Bulls Island along with Poppa's father. All my life, Poppa promised to take me to see their graves, but somehow we never made it. Once I went with a group of kids on a Sunday school outing to Big Bulls but the mosquitoes deterred us from traveling as far as the gravesite. I finally went on the Bulls Bay ferry with my brother Andrew, and was able to see the graves. We recently erected a permanent monument at the site so that their existence would always be remembered. Poppa wanted to be buried on Big Bulls beside his family, but Momma and my brothers overruled this at his death, and he was buried in Mount Pleasant Memorial Gardens. While Poppa loved my momma very much, he always loved to tell me about his first wife and the big bonnets she wore.

He loved women to wear hats, which was something my momma always did when she attended church during the school year. Poppa met and married Momma when she was eighteen and he was forty-two. My grandfather, Daniel Legare, ran the oyster factory at Shellmore. Poppa commercially harvested oysters and clams and barged them to the factory for sale, and he purchased shells there for replanting. Poppa and Momma had been married for forty-three, often stormy but always solid, years at the time of his death. Poppa was really easygoing and did not believe in spanking us girls. Whenever we did some ill deed for which Momma felt we deserved a spanking, we ran and hid behind him to find refuge from Momma's salt-water cedar switches. Momma's temper, on the other hand, was easily provoked, especially when she thought Poppa didn't take her side on an issue. She would fuss and fuss, but could hardly ever rouse a fight with Poppa, because he just wouldn't respond, even though his Scotch-Irish temper was visible at times. Once he punched a toolbox because the top fell on his head; then he could not use his hand for about a week. Poppa did not tolerate any backtalk from the boys, however. Anytime they felt they were big enough to make their own choices and argued with Poppa about his directives, he invited them out into the yard. He proceeded to wrestle with them until they were bettered and lying on the ground. Poppa was highly respected and loved by all of us, as well as the yachtsmen who frequented the island waterways.

My sister Lilly was always a part of our island family. She was mentally challenged with the IQ of a ten-year-old. She had been sent to school until second grade, and the teachers said she just could not learn, so she was taken out. It was never known whether her handicap was from birth, or the time she fell off the back steps

and split her skull. Lilly had a manner of rocking back and forth on her feet as she talked with you. She had fallen off the dock as a child and broken her ankle, and it bothered her a lot. Several people tried to convince Poppa to put Lilly into a home, but he would not even think of it, and I cannot imagine her not being a part of my life. She loved to play cards like "Old Maid" or "Go Fishing" with us, and she would accompany us as the adult to supervise our swimming, even though she did not know how to swim herself. She was the second born, which made her about eighteen years older than me. Lilly could be gentle at times, but was also hotheaded and very stubborn. One definitely did not want to get on her bad side, because he/she would receive the biggest "Charlie Horse" ever. She could really wallop you when she was angry. Once when Momma and Poppa had gone to the mainland, Earl would not relent from teasing Lilly, so she threw a brick at him. You could only push her so far!

Through the years, I learned that what worked best with Lilly was reverse psychology and positive reinforcement. She hated to take a bath, but if you told her how pretty she was going to be for her "boyfriend," she would humbly oblige. She would let me wash and fix her hair then try out different make-up techniques. Lilly moved to Mount Pleasant with Momma several years after Poppa died, and she and Momma were both diagnosed as diabetics, so I saw her almost every day when I went to administer their insulin shots. We lost Lilly at age sixty from a heart attack, which was totally unexpected. I know that she is singing up in heaven today with the angels, something she also loved to do.

My brothers, Bucky and Jimmy, were both lovers of the bottle, and it affected their personalities in totally different ways. Jimmy would become very melancholy and depressed, while Bucky's disposition became jovial and talkative. As long as I can recall, their drinking was always an issue in our family. They did not inherit their love for drinking from Poppa, because he only partook for medicinal purposes. I am told, however, that my paternal grandfather used to ride his horse down Bulls Beach so drunk that he fell off. Drinking led to an early death for Jimmy at age twenty-eight, prior to the deaths of my parents. Jimmy was cleaning a rifle and accidentally (or so it was relayed) shot himself while at the island with Poppa. I was a senior in high school, and many people thought I favored Jimmy a great deal. Bucky, who had a heart murmur from rheumatic fever passed away at age forty-four, dying before Momma. He had never gotten married because of a trauma from his teens. It is hard to understand why some lives have to bear so much trial and tribulation, but Bucky was one of those who did. It is easier to understand why he turned to drinking, but I wish someone had been able to turn him to Jesus instead. Bucky was a great teaser, and I'll always remember he gave me my first very own doll, which I loved. Because we were relatively poor, most of the gifts we received, like my first bike or big doll were shared with my sister. Individual gifts usually came from a relative like Aunt Isabel, Momma's sister who worked downtown at Kress's 5 and 10. Bucky also was the one who set the seine on the beach with Poppa for the last time and witnessed his death. He had to lift Poppa from the water and into the boat then ferry him over to the mainland and call the ambulance. He told us, "I talked to him the whole way; even though I knew he was dead, I didn't want to believe it." He then had to travel back to the island to get Momma and tell her about Poppa. I was twenty-one when Poppa died and had my first baby. Momma had always said she prayed that he would live to see me grown, and God fulfilled that prayer beyond her dream. The summer before his death, Robert and I took our five-month-old baby, Al, to the island for a visit. Poppa loved children so very much; he could not bear to see them cry. We always put Al in the playpen and let him whine himself to sleep, but before he'd had a chance, Poppa had him up in his arms and out on the screen porch in the rocker singing him to sleep. It is a wonderful last memory of my poppa that I will always cherish.

My sister Anne (Virgie to us) joined the Air Force after high school, but after nine months, she left to get married. Virgie took lessons on the piano we had in the living room at Sullivan's Island, but Marcia was the one gifted to play by ear. Without ever having a lesson, she learned to invent the most delightful tunes. Perhaps her talent was inherited from Poppa, who played the banjo with great skill, though he never had a lesson either.

Junior, being the oldest, was always relied upon heavily for advice whenever Poppa had any business decision to make. Junior was a very successful shrimper, and an even more successful businessman, though his success was built from a life of hard work. Shrimpers do not have much of a family life during the shrimping season, rising at 3:00 a.m. and getting home at dark. Today, the larger boats allow shrimpers to anchor out two or three days, and sometimes a week at a time. Junior started with one small shrimp boat and advanced until he owned a fleet of five boats. He built his home in Mount Pleasant just across from The Common. Once he was able to advance in business, the home was rented by one of his sons, and he built an even nicer brick home. Eventually, he owned three homes within the same block, one in which he allowed Momma and Lilly to live until their deaths. He also owned a dock on Shem Creek. Poppa and Momma were very proud of Junior.

I asked Junior what was one of the memories he remembered most about the island, and he said it was the time the deer flies were so bad that Poppa asked him to build a fire in the marsh. He gathered the dried sedge grass and doused it with a bit of gasoline, then threw a lit match on the pile. The fire did not ignite for some reason, so he doused it a second time with gas, and when he did, the flames shot out, scalding him all over his legs and arms, which became badly blistered. I guess that each of us has a tale of some similar type injury. I singed my eyebrows off once by trying to light the gas stove in the kitchen. Gas is not one of my favorite sources of energy for that same reason. It can be very dangerous given the right circumstances!

Junior, weathered by life and the sea, developed a very colorful way of speaking, which is how he will be remembered by many. He spoke his mind to everyone with no consideration of personal injury to the hearer. Even with his tough exterior, he had a good heart, and he was loved by many people. Diabetes and the loss of his leg took his life in 2003, but he was faithful to his profession as a fisherman until the very end. His legacy will be remembered by many, and his contributions to the industry will be treasured.

"GIGGING"

After the moon draws the sea to the
Foot of the oyster banks and darkness
Is thick like mud, Captain Clarence
Guides the bateau along the water's
Edge of Price's Inlet.
I tend the bow and he the stern
Where soot deepens the red of his
Aging eyes. He tells me the story
Of a wild boar chasing him up a tree,
And sings folk songs like "Children of
The Wild Wood." Suddenly, like a
Shark after mullet, he aims his grain*
And thrusts it at the flounder's head.
The water becomes mud thick
Where shell, bone, and steel meet.
Like a diamond jewel, he hauls
The fish into his boat, smiling
Because he has not damaged the body.
With the stars as a guide, he sets course
For home, and the silence is broken
By the gentle ripple of the oars
Dipping into the water and the
Captain's tale of a mighty haul.

*a grain is a long pole with a 4 to 5 pronged spear on the end

"MARSH-HENS"

With the air and sky crisp blue and
the tide high above the marsh,
The Captain poles his flat-bottom along
the reeds to scare up his prey.
Silence is broken only by the timely dip of
the pole splitting the sedge
As it rips the mud below and skims
the boat along the surface there.

Then a flurry of movement alerts the hunter to ready his aim,
As the marsh-hen sounds alarm and
wings his way to freedom in the air.
No match for the aged hunter,
having won this battle many times before,
His aim is steady, his shot is sure,
and quick recovery brings three birds to rest.

Though cold the day at early morning,
the thought of a hardy marsh-hen stew
Keeps him focused on the task and
the reward of bringing more birds to land.
As he strings the birds, banana-style,
he smiles, the pellets are not scattered,
And the missus will have no gripe,
as she picks clean the birds for supper.

"CATCHING MINNOWS"

"Come here, John Hue, look
What I have for you."
Fifty yellowtail minnows
Fresh caught just now.
Cracked crab in hand,
I call them to me.
They wander in my palm
To taste the dainty morsels.
Like lightning, I scoop them up
And dump them in a can.
"Most men will pay a quarter
For fifty minnows, you know."
"Eat well, my furry friend,
Tomorrow might bring no luck."

PLAYFUL LIVING

The inlet was usually quiet and peaceful, except when the yachts came up for a big weekend or a shrimp boat stopped by. When the sky turns from a radiant blue to shades of dark purple and orange, the atmosphere becomes eerie and feelings of being alone creep into my being. There is something about twilight that makes me very melancholy, and even today I have to fight the urge to get depressed at the five o'clock hour. I feel that this all stems from my experience of being alone on an island at precisely that time of day. We are all somewhat slaves to our past experiences, and it takes work to break the hold that these events have over our lives. In fact, the only true way of breaking free of "strong-holds," is to allow Jesus to take them from us. I used Psalms 56:3, "What time I am afraid, I will trust in thee" as my life verse for years. Weekends were a different story, because various yachts came up for fishing, partying, or just to relax and get away from the stress of life in the fast lane. One of the biggest weekend events for our family was the Carolina Yacht Club party. Poppa was hired to set up a big tent for them on the beach and my brothers Jimmy and Bucky, and later Andrew and Earl, would have the jobs of ferrying them

THE SLEEPY INLET

back and forth between the beaches and their boats, for which they received generous tips. Although we girls were not allowed on the beach during this big party event, I was told that the tent was for card games; and they partied heavily, evidenced by the loud music and laughter echoing across the water. Sometimes the men off the boats would get terribly drunk, and once someone had a bad accident. Typically, though, they did not get hurt if they did not try to operate their own boats after having drunk all night. I guess this is another way of saying, "don't drive and drink." After the weekend, we girls helped Poppa clean up the beach, and the best part of that was the money we found in the sand. Poppa was paid for the setup and takedown of the tent, so this was a sideline of money for our family.

Price's Inlet was our summer home, holiday home, and home away from home. Poppa stayed on the island year-round, while Momma stayed with us on Sullivan's Island to attend classes during the school year. When we were in school, we saw Poppa about once a week when he brought fish to market. He was a commercial fisherman dealing in oysters, clams, fish, and crabs. In earlier years, Poppa trapped mink and otter for their skins and sold them. These animals obviously did not remain plentiful around the coastal islands, and Poppa was forced to find other means of income. Mussels were so dense in the marshes around the island at one time that he began harvesting and shipping them to New York for sale. Mussel production grew scarce also, so later Poppa and his brother Henry worked together in the terrapin (small turtle) business, shipping crates of terrapins to New York for sale. Before shrimp boats were used for shrimping, Poppa utilized them to ferry produce from the Georgetown area to Charleston for sale, another source of income for the family. Poppa told us that many a powerful Charleston gentleman made his wealth and position by running contraband alcohol down the inland waterway during prohibition days. Schooners anchored offshore in the Atlantic, and a small boat would run out through the inlet corridor to meet the schooner where it would pick up bundled sacks of straw-wrapped bottles of alcohol, which were then transported to the mainland. Poppa himself never practiced this method of making money, but occasionally found washed up on the beach a bottle or two of the contraband, which he would deliver to some of his friends. (My brothers did occasionally hide a bit of contraband for their own personal use.)

Poppa and Momma had a list of standing customers like Henry's on Market and Carrols Seafood Market (which is now The Noisy Oyster) for oyster sales. My brothers made a living selling anything else they could catch that people would eat, including conch, shark, and mullet roe. My brother Andrew set shark lines that consisted of a heavy chain and huge hook with a float on the top end. The chain was attached to a bateau, and a "hit" was evidenced from the shore by the float bobbing up and down in the water. Many other sea creatures, such as stingray, would be caught as well. Once, when an extraordinary stingray was cut open on the dock, about twenty-five baby stingrays were inside. When the sharks were brought to the shore, they were skinned and prepared

THE SLEEPY INLET

for market. Some of the sharks captured were over ten feet in length. We swam at the dock all during our youth, not very far from where the sharks were caught, but we were never mindful of the dangers lurking just below in the deep. Of course, *Jaws* hadn't been produced then either!

Momma handpicked and opened oysters each week in the winter months when she could find someone to live at Sullivan's Island with us so she could stay Price's with Poppa. My sister Marcia often stayed with us for several months while her husband was out to sea with the navy, and when Marcia moved to Tennessee, Momma tried to find other guardians such as my brother Jimmy and his wife. In fact, I think every married brother and sister stayed at one time or another to care for those of us who were still in school. Momma shucked as many as ten gallons of oysters by herself each week. The rule of thumb for eating oysters, per Poppa, is that it is safe to eat oysters in any month containing an "R." Momma had standing orders for quarts and gallons of oysters on Broad Street, and I always loved to tag along for the deliveries because her customers like Mr. Simons would give me ten cents to buy candy at the drug store down from the First National Bank where he worked. I always chose something that would last a long time, like "Neccos." There was a really nice gentleman at the liquor store on the corner, who gave me colored beverage stirrers as a special treat. Various stops offered rewards, so I always chose to accompany Momma if she would let me. Once all of the deliveries were complete, we usually went to Robinson's Cafeteria or Woolworth's for lunch.

Momma also opened oysters for yachts that came up on weekends. Often she would open the oysters and people would eat them fresh out of the shell. She was amazing! Her fingers worked like lightning cracking the shell, rinsing the oyster, and dumping them in the cans. No one could match her speed at this task. She took orders for seafood delicacies that became a tradition, such as deviled crab, crab patties, or clam chowder. When she made deviled crab, we girls had the chore of cleaning the crab backs and picking out the crabmeat, which she inspected closely to ensure we got all the "dead men" out of the crab. Momma had food poisoning once from sea crabs, so she was especially careful in preparation for others, but never ate them again herself. I, myself, only eat stone crab, the local lobster of the crab family. I don't envision the stone crab as being as much of a scavenger as the sea crab because they live deep in a hole in oyster mud banks.

Momma also went every year to Big Bulls Beach to pick blackberries for a wonderful blackberry dumpling with a butter cream sauce. I enjoyed picking blackberries along with asparagus on Sullivan's Island where they grew wild. Today, I pick them where I can find them and make a dumpling with butter sauce at least once a year like Momma's.

BLACKBERRY DUMPLING WITH BUTTERCREAM SAUCE

Pick and wash about 4 cups of blackberries
Boil on high for about 10 minutes
Lower heat to medium
Add 2 cups of sugar
(Taste to see if more sugar needs to be added—
depends on sweetness of berries)
Cook until blackberries begin to tender
Make dumplings (either from Bisquick or use canned biscuits)
Break biscuits in half, roll in flour,
then roll out and cut in half again
Drop in dumplings when berries are almost done and cook until dumplings are fluffy.

Butter Cream Sauce
1 stick real butter
1 cup sugar
2 teaspoons vanilla
Whip well and place 1 tablespoon into a bowl of hot dumplings

OYSTER STEW

8–10 fresh medium sized oysters
1 cup heavy cream
1 cup milk
¼ stick real butter
¼ teaspoon celery salt
Salt and pepper to taste
Scald milk. Add other ingredients, and lower heat
Add oysters and simmer till oysters are done

Momma had a hard life working alongside Poppa while trying to raise eleven children. She was small of stature but unequalled when it came to energy. With her short black curly hair and her weathered and wrinkled face, she was always on the move. Because Poppa did not think material things were needed, Momma worked twice as hard to provide us with the things she never had as a child. Her love language was definitely "acts of service," because she would do anything for anyone in need. When Poppa died, she did not want to leave the island, where she lived with my sister Lilly. There were times when fishermen came up to steal a few oysters off the banks, but Momma quickly got into her boat with a shotgun and ran them off. She would give you the shirt off her back, but never try to steal it. The family finally made her and Lilly move to Mount Pleasant because it was too treacherous driving the boat across the narrow strait of the channel by herself. Deprived of her beloved island and never really getting over Poppa's death, she withdrew into her own world and spent her last several years unaware that we were her children. She was one of the most wonderful moms in the whole world, striving to give us a childhood of material things and love she did not know. She told us about the cruelty of her stepmother, who made them walk to school without shoes. Her stepmother showed favoritism to her own children, and Momma never knew the love of a real mother. She needed us to love her more and craved an embrace to signify that she was loved. Why are the simplest gestures of affection the ones we fail so often to bestow on those we love?

One of my favorite night sports was to go gigging with Poppa. I always begged Bucky, but he seldom let me go, because to him it was serious business. Gigging required that you wake up at whatever time of night low tide fell, which could be anywhere from midnight to four o'clock in the morning. The weather was considered desirable if the wind was very calm and there was no rain. It did not matter that stars were not out, the night was black like soot,

and a gas jack lantern provided the only light for fishing. We went gigging in one of the wooden bateaux Poppa made, poling our way down the oyster banks or along the beach side. Poppa used the gas jack lantern to flare out over the water and light up the spot where the fish made their bed. Gigging flounder provided another good source of income for the family. I recall nights when Bucky gigged as many as one hundred and fifty flounder in the days before it was illegal and fishing licenses were unheard of. Poppa, a true conservationist, was very specific about the way you speared a flounder, indicating that you should always aim for the head so as not to mess up the body. He believed in taking just what you needed to survive and leaving some for another day. He got angry because the boys caught too many fish. There were times out in the black night that I questioned whether we would make it back home safely because I had no sense of direction in that pitch dark. Poppa, on the other hand, steered the boat in the perfect direction, just like a horse heading for the barn. He could find his way home from any creek no matter what the condition. The grains used for gigging were made by Poppa and the prongs were sharpened on the grinder kept under the shed at the dock. Once the catch was brought in, the fish were stored in the icehouse until time to take them to market. Once or twice a week Poppa or my brothers would have to make a trip to the mainland, crossing at Buck's Farm (now Bulls Bay Golf Club), then traveling to Mount Pleasant to get large blocks of ice for fish preservation on the island.

In the fifties, we purchased ice from the supplier at the corner of Rifle Range Road (now Mathis Ferry) and Pitt Street in Mount Pleasant. Poppa covered the ice blocks with a croker sack to keep the ice from melting too much until reaching the island. Once we arrived at the island, the ice was hoisted by ice tongs from the boat to the icehouse and again covered with a croker sack to slow the melting process. Most of my brothers were very strong, as it took quite a bit of strength to lift the solid blocks of ice from the boat and up the hill to the icehouse. If there were fish to be stored in the icehouse, a block of ice was chipped up into a wooden crate, and the fish were nestled therein with a croker sack as their blanket. Prior to purchase of a gas refrigerator, milk and other commodities were stored in the icehouse along with the fish, which often gave them a strong fishlike smell. Anytime ice was needed for the dinner tea, one of us had to make the trip to the landing to retrieve a bowlful. The smell of the ice often deterred one's desire to drink milk or other beverages. However, fresh milk was a better choice than "Clem," my Momma's favorite powdered milk drink. Those were the days when milk was really fresh and came in glass bottles. At our home it was considered a delicacy, and the heavy cream sitting about an inch from the cap was gleaned off to use in Poppa's coffee. No food or drink was wasted in our household. If the milk ever spoiled, it was allowed to clabber and was then eaten with sugar. The taste somewhat resembles that of cottage cheese. It was one of my poppa's favorite dishes.

SETTING THE SEINE

Setting the seine on the beach was one of Poppa's most enjoyable methods of catching fish and one of the most productive as well. Bulls Beach had a very large slew, and Poppa set stakes out across the mouth of the entrance. When tide was high, the seine was attached to the top of the stakes, and large pieces of rocks were set at the bottom to hold the seine in place. As the tide went out, the fish were trapped inside the slew, and Poppa would let us run up and down to chase them into the net. You could also walk in the shallow spots and gig the flounder that lay camouflaged in their beds. Often stingrays would get caught in the slew and sometimes a small shark. Poppa would allow us to swim along beside the boat and put the rocks on the bottom for him. Once while helping Poppa, I was stung over fifty times by jelly fish, which caused a very high fever. I believe all of my brothers had enjoyed setting the seine with Poppa as well. One time proved to be too much for all of us, however.

Poppa was eighty-three, and he had suffered a slight stroke. The stroke left no outwardly visible signs of injury; however, his heart had been damaged. The doctors told him not to do anything very strenuous—but try keeping a lion in a cage for very long. Poppa was determined to enjoy the experience he loved so much at least one more time. He took my brother Bucky and set the seine once more, but the feat would prove to be too much for him. He had a heart attack that very day and died, falling into the waters in the Big Bulls slew that he loved so much. Even in this, we saw God's blessing, as he was taken in an instant with no suffering, doing his life's work. I was only twenty-one years old, yet I still recall Robert coming to tell me about it. I was not ready to let him go, nor were any of us, because he was the essence of all you could hope for in an earthly father. His death was hardest on my brother Bucky however, because he was the one who had to lift his body into the boat, take him to the mainland, call the emergency vehicle, then go back to the island to tell my momma. I don't believe that Bucky or my momma ever got over this experience.

Eventually, tidal currents causing erosion and resettlement of the sands changed the shape of the beach, and the slew disappeared. At one time, the beach was almost cut in half. Geological studies of the area began to be done by Clemson University each summer and later by the Army Corps of Engineers. I suppose it is just as well, because seining later became an illegal method of fishing.

MARSH-HENNING AND FIDDLERING

During the seasonally high marsh-hen tides, Poppa would often charter a group from one of the yachts and pole across the marshes for the sport of shooting marsh-hens. Whenever he did, he always brought back a string of the birds for Momma to make a stew. We had to pick the birds clean; then Momma would stew them down in brown gravy that was really delicious. The only irritating thing about eating the birds was biting down on one of the pellets that somehow went undetected during the cleaning process. It has been many years since I had marsh-hen, and I don't know if I would eat it today, but I do love a good orange-glazed duck. Marsh-hen is a meat that is generally considered more of a "poor man's dish." I do not believe many people actually participate in this sport anymore.

As kids, we made pocket money for sweets from the mainland by catching fiddler crabs or minnows, which we sold to the yachtsmen to use for fishing bait. Fiddlers were not one of my favorite things to capture, and I always avoided the ones with really large claws. You have to grab fiddlers by the back, then pinch off their large claw and toss them into a bucket of saltwater to keep them alive. Sheepshead fish especially love the fiddler crab, but they only bite on china-back fiddlers. Fishermen used the minnows for bass or flounder fishing. They were caught by cupping a small piece of crab or bread in your hands underwater and softly chanting, "here minnow, minnow, minnow." As the minnows swarmed to taste the delicacies, you had to quickly close your palms tightly together. It was easy to capture five or six minnows at a time. The tiny fish were also a delicacy for our feral cats, which were abundant on the island. One special cat we all adored was "John Hue" who loved to skirt around the pilings surrounding the dock. One particularly cold winter day, he fell into the water and never recovered from the shock.

We met some really nice people from the yachts that visited the island who hired us to catch bait for them. One of my fondest memories is of Mr. Thornhill who had one of the largest house yachts that visited. Each summer he brought a group of Clemson students up for a long weekend. A jovial man always full of teasing, Mr. Thornhill once took my sister and me out to his yacht in the inlet for a treat. We were under a magical spell watching the dumb waiter bring us a Coke up from the galley below—we did not know such conveniences existed. He promised me that if I would attend Clemson College when I grew up, he would pay for my college, but he became sick and stopped coming to the island before I was ready for college. Because Poppa really did not have the money to send me to college, I went to business school upon graduating from high school. Later, I put myself through college and graduated from the College of Charleston in 1983. My son Al did graduate from Clemson, however, so I wonder if this might count in my stead.

We also made money for spending by doing chores Poppa assigned to us such as picking buckets of oysters or clams or heading buckets of shrimp. He paid us twenty-five cents a bucket. Inflation never caught on with Poppa because he paid me the same amount to head shrimp he paid my sisters ten and twelve years earlier to pick buckets of oysters. Sometimes he paid us ten cents to bail out bateaux after a heavy rain or to help him paint a chair or bateau he had finished. He believed in teaching the work ethic that we should all earn our way, and so he paid us for most of what we were asked to do for him, but never for household chores. Household jobs were Momma's department, and she assigned us each chores, which if not done resulted in a switching, and they had better be done to her liking. Many a night Poppa would ask one of us to wash his feet before he retired to bed. He would offer to pay ten cents for this chore as well, but I never took the money because I loved doing this for Poppa. This reminded me of Jesus washing the feet of His disciples. What a blessing to be able to humble oneself to serve someone in such a manner.

OLD JOE

Although I never actually saw Old Joe, I remember the picture on Momma and Poppa's bedroom wall of the majestic pelican camped atop the creosote post down at the dock. Old Joe had somehow managed to break a wing, and Poppa had found him and nursed him back to health. Thereafter, he lived at the dock, leaving for short bouts to scout out a fresh meal but always returning to the post he called home. Through the years of hearing about Poppa's love for Old Joe and seeing his picture, I, too, grew to have a special love for pelicans. They command a certain air of authority and magnificence that many other birds just do not have. If you ever manage to make a friend of one, he will be your friend for life. Whenever Poppa got into the bateau to row across to the beach or into one of the creeks for fishing, Old Joe perched himself on the front of the boat and went along for the ride. Poppa saved fish to feed Old Joe, and yet this did not spoil his adjustment to the wild. He remained capable of taking care of his own meal anytime he chose.

"OLD JOE"

How stately is your pose, my friend.
How majestically you rest so bold
Atop the creosote post
You've chosen to call home.

Though you may venture out
To catch a tasty fish for meal,
You always wander back this way.
What is this unnatural bond you feel?

For a bird has no soul or heart
To love as people do.
Yet by this friendship we have made
Nature reveals another side of you.

THE LIVELIHOOD

Picking oysters was one of my family's biggest businesses, and one of the hardest. Oysters were sold in a bushel croker sack, in either clusters or selects (singles) or opened by the quart or gallon. At one time, the business was large enough that Poppa barged the oysters to the factory for sale, but during my childhood, mostly weekly orders were taken for individual customers or businesses. There were two wonderful black guys who helped for a long period of time, Border and Henry. In fact, I affectionately called them both "uncle" and would always get them to bring me candy from Creech's Country Store when coming over from the mainland. Because Poppa was born in the late eighteen hundreds, he was accustomed to segregation and referred to blacks as "darkies," and whenever Border or Henry shared a meal, they always sat on the back steps of the porch while we ate at the table, something with which I never grew comfortable. If I invited them in to the table, Henry would say, "We'se fine right here, missie."

Gathering oysters and clams is accomplished during the coldest months of the year. I can still see Momma with her stretch knit cap, overalls, hip boots and heavy jacket. She walked the banks, choosing the mature oysters, and with a crow iron, the undesirable portions were lopped off. First, she would row to the banks that were ripe for harvest, scaling the banks, and then the oysters were picked and thrown into the bateau. Once a good haul was accomplished, she would row back to the island where the oysters were stored on oyster racks until bagged and ready to deliver to market. Later this practice was questioned by the Wildlife Department, which made my brother Junior very angry. He did not feel they had the authority to come on to private property and make demands. Their methods upset my brother Andrew, so Junior went to the house, got his rifle, and ordered them off the land. I won't elaborate on the consequences, but suffice to say many pounds of shrimp were donated to charity. I can bet you if Poppa had been alive, he would have done the same thing.

Our family leased approximately two hundred acres of oyster lands surrounding the island, and Poppa planted the beds in rotation as needed. Oysters require a great deal of work to actually get them growing. An empty shell is planted in the mud bank, and an irritation causes the oyster to begin forming in the shell. The upper shell begins to form until the oyster reaches maturity. At one point in time, shells were purchased from the oyster factory for replanting, but most of the factories in the area closed. Seed oysters were then introduced; they were planted in shallow creek beds and transferred to fertile areas for growth. This process soon ceased, as seed oysters were no longer available. Because of the demise of oyster factories and seed oyster production, and probably because oyster shells became a commodity for many other uses, shells for replanting became scarce. Today, the oyster industry in the low country is dying, and no one can really figure out why. My brother Andrew, who took up the gauntlet of picking oysters, attributes it to the high number of motorboats and the pollution they cause. The business has become even more costly, as hundreds of stakes have to be planted on the banks to help with erosion. Once this

has been accomplished, all the banks have to be inspected. Many oysters have a small orange soft crab inside, and some people, including my brother Earl, like to eat them. Whenever Momma opened oysters and found a crab inside, Earl would pop it into his mouth and let it crawl around on his tongue before chewing it up and swallowing. He delighted in doing this before spectators who oohed and aahed at this feat. When the oyster business was at its peak, we had an oyster house that was inspected by the health department to insure it was in good condition for packaging and public sale. Momma would crack the oysters on an anvil (a wooden block with an iron rod out the top.) Her skill at doing this was unmatched by anyone, and many of the yacht people loved to just sit and watch her perform. I'm sure it was hard for her to see what she was doing, because the oyster shell debris was always splashing all over her glasses, and she could not see anything without them.

Our family also harvested clams, but not to the degree that it is being done today. Clams were planted in a shallow mud bank when they were tiny seedlings and transplanted to more fertile

and deeper creek waters for growth. Clams had a poor rate of survival at one time because of a predator known as the clam cracker. It destroyed tremendous numbers of clam beds. It was such a threat that Poppa set stakes in and around the beds to try to keep the clam crackers away. In more recent years, the clam crackers have virtually disappeared, probably due to the shrimping industry, and clams are much more plentiful. In earlier days, they were harvested by hand rake in shallow beds and a set of tongs in deeper waters, but today most of the harvesting is done by hydraulic machinery.

My brother Andrew still clams the old-fashioned way, but enjoys an income from the hydraulic harvesting as well. The clams harvested are not often found in the local restaurants but are shipped to other cities. Baby clams steamed and dipped in butter is a dish that is hard to beat. Pepper clams are a recently developed breed; they are tiny, with etched backs and a naturally spicy flavor.

Harvesting crabs was a unique business. Momma made crab dishes that were sold to the yachtsmen who came up for weekend stays at Price's. We did have a few crab traps; though they were not as plentiful in the late forties and fifties as they are today. The stone crabs were the hardest to trap, and more were caught at night by gigging off the oyster banks than any other way. My brothers had a unique skill of reaching their arm deep into the mud hole where the crab lay, and pulling it out without getting bitten. The trick is to catch the crab from behind, because in the hole, he cannot open his claws, but once he's outside, you're fair game! There was also a small iron claw bar that was used to draw the crab out of the hole. Once, my brother Bucky teased me with a live, snipping crab from his plentiful batch, and it unfortunately latched onto my finger. There is an old tale that once a stone crab latches on, he won't let go until it thunders. We made all kinds of noises, but to no avail. Finally, the crab had to be killed to get it off my finger. Today, I still have a knot on my left index finger as a reminder not to get too close to a live stone crab.

Poppa purchased the family's first shrimp boat, the *Geneva Moore* which was mainly used to deliver vegetables. He subsequently sold this to Uncle Henry. Next he purchased the *Ruth*, which he and my brother shrimped for many years then Poppa sold it to Junior. Poppa also helped my brothers, Dan and Andrew, purchase their first shrimp boat, The *Hope* which Andrew owned and then sold to Dan. Andrew continued to share ownership of his boat, the *Playboy*, with Momma and Poppa until their deaths. We also had a small inboard boat called the *Black Boat*, which Poppa purchased from a gentleman that worked for the Department of Health and Environmental Control. This was used occasionally for shrimping, but it was mostly used for trips to the mainland via the inland waterway. When making this passage, we often stopped by Goat Island. The Goat Man and his wife came to the edge of the water and Poppa would stop to give them some supplies. Growing up, I always thought that we were poor, but being poor is always relative, because to us, the Goat Man was poor.

OLD-FASHIONED REMEDIES

Momma's homemade remedies were a real trip. Because we were a large family, we did not go to the doctor for everything that came up, also perhaps because there was not one readily available. It took a boat ride of several hours to get to the doctor for any sickness or injury. Once after supper, my sister Tommy and I chased each other outside trying to be the first to the tree swing. Unfortunately, I didn't see the board with the rusty nail protruding, and the nail stuck deep into my foot. Because it was almost dark, a trip to the mainland was out of the question, so Momma bathed it with Epsom salt. The next morning I had a red streak running up my leg and Momma told Poppa to get the *Black Boat* ready to take me directly down the inland waterway to the doctor. Doctor Picket, a local Pitt Street doctor, said I would have gotten lockjaw if I had not made it there within a few more hours for my tetanus shot. Incidents like this were not uncommon. Another time, I slit my leg open playing ship on a log covered with oyster shells. The wound was rather large, and I still have a big scar, because it probably needed stitches that were unavailable on the island.

Poppa was never in the hospital one day of his life, though he got occasional colds. The treatment was "Walmpose Preparation"or "Peptonoid Creosote" and another dark drug called "Asafetida", which had a strong smell of rotten onions. According to family lore the name is derived from German and means "devil dung." which should give some hint to its potency. Also, Momma would often make a strange concoction of hot water, orange/lemon peels, onions, and sugar, which you had to drink for a cold. Yuck, yuck, yuck is all I have to say about that! My parents were not drinkers, except on special occasions or for medicinal purposes. Poppa would keep a bottle of rock and rye laced with rock candy or peaches, and if he had been picking oysters on a really cold day, he would have a sip. Momma would make a hot toddy from about a tablespoon of whiskey, sugar, hot water, and lemon peels to help with cramps or a really bad flu. The secret is to get under a bunch of blankets, and drink the potion slowly until you break a sweat and the fever breaks—then you feel much better.

Once I decided to get an overall tan, which was something easy to do with no other people living on the island. I went out behind the pump shed to lay atop the oyster shells with only my sunglasses on, and I read until I fell fast asleep. Lilly came and woke me up, but by that time, I was burned so badly that I peeled in layers. I tried all of Momma's suggestions for treating sunburn from raw potato peelings to rubbing aloe plants on my body. I had to wear a T-shirt under my clothes for days because I could not stand for anything rough to touch my skin. Needless to say, I learned my lesson about nude sun-bathing. Another thing Momma always made sure of was that we had a dose of worm medicine every six months. She gave us "Vermifuge", which made you want to puke, but if you did, you got another dose, so it was best to hold your nose and stomach it the first time. There was always a bottle of Milk of Magnesia in the medicine closet in case of constipation. Momma made her own special Octagon soap too, which was used for washing clothes, our bodies, and our hair. She was very particular about us being clean and made sure we did not have head lice; she felt the Octagon soap was a good deterrent for that. Momma used to say, "We might be poor, but we can always be clean." She made sure we always wore clean undergarments without holes in the event we were in an accident.

A tremendously annoying body ailment I remember having as a small child was "boils." A boil is an extremely painful and inflamed swelling of the skin with a large white core in the middle that oozes pus. Momma used a black salve ointment, called Ichthyol, to cover the boil and then bandaged the area to try to draw out the core. Sometimes, when it was about ready, Momma would make us sit while she squeezed and we yelled, until the core popped out. I have never discovered what exactly causes boils, but Momma always said it was "bad blood." So if we got a boil, we got a boost of a proper diet, no sweets, and a dose of Asafetida to cleanse our blood. I truly believe taking this foul medicine is one reason I still cannot stomach onions today.

Because he loved honey and enjoyed sucking on the honeycomb, Poppa also raised honey bees on the island. He had a special helmet with a screen mask he wore inside the pen where the beehive was located. If he, or any of us, ever got stung, a warm tea bag was placed on the area to draw out the stinger. It was worth a sting to be able to enjoy a hot biscuit with butter and some fresh honey. A tour guide I met once in Mexico City suggested that a teaspoon of honey each day would help to keep you free from colds. I didn't realize that Poppa's secret traveled so far! If we take a trip to the mountains, I try to find a jar of honey with the honeycomb in it so I can enjoy sucking on the wax comb.

Poppa had his own special secrets such as always producing a bountiful garden in the salty, sandy soil he cultivated each summer and winter. We grew potatoes, corn, tomatoes, squash, cucumbers, etc., and one of the things that made the garden grow so well was the dead fish he used to fertilize the soil, even though the odor was almost unbearable. Whenever we traveled past the garden, we broke out in a run until safely past the smell. One of my fondest memories was digging potatoes in that garden. It is something I have always loved to do. My brother Andrew still produces a wonderful crop each year and shares the vegetables among the family.

The cedar trees on the island were always plagued by a worm that lived inside a tough-skinned cocoon. Poppa would pay us to pick them off the trees, after which he would burn them. Worms are not one of my favorite creatures, and I recall one particular day when the *Seahawk* was visiting at the dock for a long weekend stay. The *Seahawk* was one of the larger cabin boats that came for weekends at Price's. The captain often rented the cottage Poppa built for that purpose. As a child, I was intrigued by the *Seahawk*, and I thought it was, along with Mr. Thornhill's yacht, one of the largest boats I had ever seen. Their cook, Spike, was also one of my favorites, as he would always save us some of the dessert he made for dinner, and homemade ice cream was a special treat. On this particular trip, one of the owners' wives, Mrs. Fanny Middleton, wanted me to run from the dock to the house to get Momma, so she could talk with her about a special dish they wanted Momma to prepare. Mrs. Middleton was a wonderfully exciting person, always vivacious and adorned with the neatest hats, which she often passed down to Momma when she grew tired of them. She promised to give me a special treat upon my return from giving Momma the message. I ran as fast as I could, excited to get back and retrieve my prize; so you can imagine my chagrin when I was handed a napkin, and wrapped inside was a French-fried worm. She explained that they had enjoyed the delicacies for supper, and she just knew I was going to love it. All I could think about was the worms I picked off the cedar trees. "No one would believe people really ate worms as food," I thought, as I gently wrapped the worm back in the napkin to save and show all my friends. Since that time, I have watched as the participants on the popular reality show "Survivor" bravely downed live specimens of the squirming, crunchy delicacies. I guess if things get bad enough, some people will eat anything—but not me!

MARY MAGWOOD CAUSEY

"FRIED WORMS"

Picking worms can be great fun.
Squeeze the cocoon to watch them squirm,
Rolling into a little ball,
That's why they're called a worm?

Could you imagine one French- fried,
Like shrimp in sherry, dipped bread?
Total elegance, like snails and such
Things about which you've only read.

Like a gem in a napkin, one was
Given to me as a prize.
I opened the wondrous gift,
And could not take it from my eyes.

Who would eat a worm from a tree
Even if camouflaged quite well?
It's something I would fear to do
Lest I not live to tell.

THE SLEEPY INLET

"OLD-TIME REMEDIES"

"Old-Time Remedies"
What has the world come to?
Aspirin and antibiotics galore,
Special creams and ointments
To cure an itch or a sore

Medicines once were scarce,
And the best cures were free,
For treating things like head lice
Or the sting from a bee.

Octagon soap for the lice,
Hot tea bags for the sting,
Boiled onion with lemon and water
To cure colds or most anything!

When a cut is infectious
Or a nail breaks the skin,
Soak in hot Epsom salt
For a sure fire win.

Try turpentine for red bugs,
Not internally, though;
Clorox to bath water
Will not let them grow.

When your blood is sluggish,
And you're feeling quite low,
A teaspoon of honey
Will keep you on the go.

Old-fashioned remedies,
Like old-fashioned ways,
Are still the best ones
In these modern-life days.

TALL TALES

THE PLAT-EYE

Walking down the beach in the early evening dusk, you might just spot a plat-eye lying in the sand. Plat-eyes are pitch black, hard-surfaced pieces of dried eggs from a type of sting ray with two whisker-like extensions off each end and measuring around the size of a half-dollar coin. Legend says that the name plat-eye comes from a huge monster similar to Bigfoot with one huge eye in the middle of his head. The plat-eye is actually the egg that is supposed to be one of the eyes from the monster. He stalks the beach at night looking for prey and for his lost eye that is buried somewhere in the sand. If you should get caught out on a desolate beach at night, beware the plat-eye. When I was a young girl my brothers taunted us with this saying, and I was totally freaked out. Any time we were on the beach in late afternoon, I could not rest until we were safely in the boat and on the way back to our island. I begged for us to leave as early as possible, and I never wanted to venture too near the larger sand dunes close to the woods where Momma went to pick blackberries. Besides my fear of the plat-eye, there was always a chance of a wild boar or some other wild animal appearing out of the thicket and attacking anything in its path. In fact, that very thing happened to Momma once. She and Poppa were on Capers Beach, early in its season, when the woods were much thicker and dead trees did not line its banks. As they walked the beach, looking for trash to call treasure, a wild boar came darting out of the woods at them. Momma said Poppa immediately climbed the nearest tree, leaving her to fend for herself. She had to go far out into the ocean to avoid the menace. Even today, tales of the "plat-eye" manage to keep the younger ones close at foot.

"THE PLAT-EYE"

At dark of night
When the sun don't shine
Look about the shore
For a plat-eye sign.

Coal-black like soot
And hard as a bat
Whiskers out each side
A lot like a cat

Buried in the sand,
It waits for its prey.
The eye from the beast
Is what they say!

Bigger than "Big Foot"
And meaner than a snake
Don't let it catch you
For goodness sake!

TIGER BILL

Old Bill was a wonderful and very large, old black gentleman who visited the island and worked with my parents for many years; he had his own temporary abode built atop creosote posts, which later became one of Poppa's tool sheds. Old Bill rowed a bateau across from Tiger Creek when he worked by the day, thereby the nickname by which he was affectionately known—"Tiger Bill." It is said that the yacht people got a thrill out of trying to get him drunk. They would hand him a glass of whiskey, which he would down without batting an eye and never sway a bit. We really never knew Old Bill's age, but he died when my sister Marcia was around twelve, about the time I was born. What I learned about him came from my older brothers and sisters. Old Bill was so loved and trusted by my parents that he was put in charge of us when they both had to leave the island for the mainland to take a catch to market. He did the cooking in Momma's absences as well—like when she was in bed with another baby, which was about every other year. He made the best cornbread in an old-fashioned iron skillet baked in a wood oven. My brother Junior recalls him teasing as he cooked, "Watch me flip 'em liken doze fancy cooks downtown," and he would proceed to flip the cornbread, with half landing in the skillet and half on the stove. My sister Marcia said that when she was a baby she was very hard to put to sleep, and Old Bill would tell Momma, "Give her'n to me, Ise'll gets her to sleep." He would then gently rock her back and forth on his knee while smoking his pipe and singing Gullah tunes to her. Gullah is a dialect of the black people who settled here, and it is still spoken in parts of Johns Island, McClellanville, and in other rural areas of the low country. Momma said it worked every time! I'll bet he and Poppa had a time together, Poppa playing his banjo and singing and jiving with Old Bill. Poppa had many tunes that we loved to sing with him. He'd laugh as Momma forbade him to sing certain words that would be considered common talk in today's open culture.

"FAVORITES ON THE BANJO"

Children of the Wild Wood
Children of de sea
Children of de low ground
Where nobody be!

Shrow dat Hook
In de middle of de pond
Catch dat girl
With de red dress on
I'll be dog if I can see
How dat girl
Got away from me.

Sheep and the Nanny Goat
Walking in de pasture
Sheep say ta nanny goat
Walk a little faster.

Sheep's milk and goat's dung
Make a mighty plaster,
Put 'em on de sheep's tail
And make 'em walk faster.

Old Bill was such a part of the island that even after his death, his presence seemed to linger. It became a legend that his ghost inhabited his old house, and sometimes he would be seen walking the path to the dock. My brother Earl and my sister Tommie taunted me with this many a time as I ran behind them trying to keep up. They would yell, "Watch out, Old Bill's going to get ya." By the time I made it to the house I was always shaking and crying from fear that he was close behind and ready to do something horrible to me. My brothers enjoyed taunting tremendously because whenever we had a shrimp boat visiting the island, they would tease the black men who worked with them about Old Bill as well. Their eyes would get wide with fright and they refused to go back to the boat unless one of my brothers accompanied them into the dark night. If only then we had known to call "Ghost Busters!" If the workers or I had known Old Bill, we would never have been afraid in the first place. Even today, my brother believes that ghosts inhabit the island. He swears that he has seen my momma in and around the island.

TRIPS TO THE MAINLAND

In the late 1940s, a trip to town was a major ordeal. First, the family had to row across the inland waterway passage to Buck's Farm then catch a Greyhound bus to Charleston. Once we arrived at Buck's Farm, we had to walk a couple of miles out to Highway 17 to the local grocery store/gas station to wait on the bus. The walk was given an added dimension of excitement when one of the farm bulls was out in the pasture. My heart almost beat out of my chest as we tried to make it past the bull without setting off his alarm.

Until the family purchased its first vehicle, we had to walk to the farm shed to call someone to pick us up. An old pickup, which was generally left at Buck's Farm, was purchased in the fifties to make it easier to haul the catch to market. Since neither Momma nor Poppa ever learned to drive, one of us did the driving for the family. Whether you wanted to get your license or not, you were encouraged to do so. In fact, it was a necessity! I learned to drive an old stick shift truck and got my license at age fourteen, mainly because someone was needed to pick Momma and Poppa up when they made trips to the mainland. I don't think Bucky, Jimmy, Earl, or Tommie ever learned to drive.

The trip across the inlet was often treacherous in the small open bateau. Larger yachts traveled the inland waterway making large wakes, which sometimes threatened to capsize our small boat. Many times, we had to bail furiously to rid the boat of the water resulting from the large waves lapping over the sides. Add to this a blustery day when the wind caused whitecaps, and you can imagine the fear flowing through our hearts at the thought of not making it home.

Some good things came from these mainland crossings and one was quality time. I loved to sit beside Poppa and steer the boat. He did not trust that I could handle it alone, so he always sat beside me to instruct in the event I strayed too far left or right. The passage was staked out to avoid oyster banks hidden beneath the water, and if the tide was less than full high tide, one had to be very careful not to go out of bounds. One particular time, Poppa and I were traveling across from Buck's Farm to the island, and I sat telling him about things at school and asking questions about his early life. He gently laid his hand on top of my thigh and said, "Mame', the boys don't put their hands there, do they?" I answered without hesitation, "No way, Poppa!" Just to make certain, he further instructed me that I should never let a boy do that. Poppa was really old-fashioned. Marcia said once when she went on a date at Sullivan's Island Poppa was there when she arrived home waiting on the porch with a crow bar.

Whenever Momma and Poppa took trips to town to take fish to market, we always liked to go along. Sometimes Momma would not care, and other times she was determined that no kids would be allowed to make the trip. I hated to have to stay on the island when they were gone. I begged to be allowed to go, and Momma would relent only if Poppa gave money for new shoes or a dress for school. Poppa usually obliged, but Momma still would not be coerced even then. Once I hid under a stack of croaker sacks being carried to cover the ice on the return trip. I thought I would pop out when we were too far along for them to take me back to the island, but it didn't work. I could not stand the loneliness inside when both Momma and Poppa were gone overnight, sometimes for two days. It was those times when I climbed the steps to the attic over and over, looking for that small black speck moving slowly along the waterway that signified they were on the way home. One had to watch very carefully to determine that the speck was a boat and not a bird. To this day, while I like space in my surroundings, I do not like to be totally alone for very long.

When the boat returned to the dock, we had to make sure we were there to help carry supplies back to the house. We used a wheelbarrow to haul the groceries and usually a treat Poppa brought back. One of his favorites was a large box of Sugar Daddies or Fireballs, which were quickly hidden (or so they thought) in Momma and Poppa's chiffonier. If we wanted one, we had to ask Momma's permission, which might or might not be given, strictly by whim. Bottled drinks were a real rarity. The few drinks we got were Nehi beverages, which Poppa liked so much. Two of his favorites were ginger and strawberry, and ginger fast became a favorite of mine. The bottles were always saved for the refund; and losing one could mean a spanking because ten cents went a long way in those days.

HOLIDAYS

Each year when school got out for Christmas holidays, we went to the island for the entire vacation. When I was in school, we had Christmas first on Sullivan's Island where we cut a tree from the wooded backyard area of our home. I do not ever remember actually celebrating Christmas day itself on the island, although we may have when I was very small. Marcia said that when they were little, she remembers their one gift being on the mantle on Christmas morning. Once Poppa cut a salt-water cedar tree, which was decorated with handmade paper ornaments; that is the only time my sisters recall having an actual tree on the island. However, Junior remembered that Momma always had one placed in the living room. She wanted the largest tree possible, and often you could barely get through the door past it. Christmas was a special time for us. We always had stockings (the largest of Poppa's boot socks we could find) hung on the fireplace for Santa to fill. On Christmas morning, these would be stuffed to the top with apples, oranges, bananas, hard candy, and a variety of shelled nuts. We never received toys in the stockings, and I am not sure when that tradition changed. Poppa did not see the need of gifts for Christmas, so

Momma had to be the one to insure we received something under the tree. Of course, that something was only one item, not several, as we are in the habit of doing for our kids today. My brother gave me my first doll, a red-haired beauty, which I kept until the rats ate it apart in the attic. Momma always crocheted each of us girls a pillow doll. She would use a plastic doll that looked something like a modern-day Barbie, then make a fan-shaped dress for the doll that would frame your pillow. These usually had very colorful dresses, and the doll's hair was red, blond, or black. I don't remember us getting gifts from each other at Christmas, but we always bought for Poppa and Momma. Poppa usually got ginger, Old Spice, suspenders, or his favorite shirt, while Momma got "Evening in Paris" perfume, Pond's cold cream, or some candy. Momma definitely had a sweet tooth, too. Poppa would always bring her special treats from the mainland that we were not allowed to touch. Unless there was some major reason why we could not go to Price's, that is where our holidays were spent. I do recall once or twice having spent them at Sullivan's Island. There we would go to through the woods to the back inlet and pick a tree, which was cut for the living room.

Christmas dinner typically consisted of roasted pork with potatoes and carrots, candied yams, corn pie, green beans, and tea. Sometimes turkey was served in lieu of the pork, but I believe we all preferred Momma's pork. There was always a variety of sweets for dessert, including Momma's divinity fudge. She made a homemade fruitcake each year, which she covered in blackberry wine to give it moisture and always, always, we had her famous cherry nut cake. The cherry nut cake is still a favorite for many of us today, and I always make and give away several at Christmas time.

At Easter, the bunny never missed our home. Easter baskets were hidden somewhere around the house and we had to hunt for them. We dyed Easter eggs with old-fashioned food coloring and hid candied marshmallow eggs in Saran Wrap. Momma made sure that we had our share of goodies and presents at each special holiday. She worked hard to give us the love and abundance in life that she never knew.

CHERRY NUT CAKE

1 lb. butter
6 cups sugar
6 cups flour
12 eggs
1 pint heavy whipping cream
6 cups chopped and floured nuts (pecans, Brazil nuts, and walnuts)
2 small jars maraschino cherries cut in half and floured
2 teaspoons vanilla
2 teaspoons lemon juice
Bake in slightly greased and floured tube pans (2)
or loaf pans (4) at 350 degrees till light brown
(Still one of our favorites)

ISLAND DREAMS

When you live on an island with no lights or TV, and little social contact, one of the most popular things to do is read. I love to read, and on the island I read everything I got my hands on, including some of Momma's copies of *True Romances*. The island influenced my creative side as well, and also made me a hopeless romantic and a dreamer. In late afternoons, when the wind died down, and the sea became so calm it seemed like you could walk on it, I walked to the dock beneath the unusually purple sky, watching boats pass the channel markers and fantasizing about the people on the yachts and where they were going. Many times I would dream of one of the yachts turning at marker 86 and coming to the island with a handsome man aboard who would sweep me hopelessly off my feet. I finally met my Lancelot in high school, not from a yacht, and he was as poor as we were. One night, however, I had a rather close encounter that left some preteen scars.

Around the age of twelve, I had been tucked in for the night, and I was lazily reading when a frantic knock came at the door. It was a scoutmaster who had brought a troop of boy scouts up for a weekend of camping on Big Bulls Beach. One of the boys had hastened too close to the oyster banks adjacent to the beach and had fallen and cut his leg open. The scoutmaster came to see what medical assistance we might give, and if we had a phone he could use but there were none. Of course, Momma offered her usual remedy, Epsom Salt in hot water. While she gently bathed the wound and prepared it for bandaging, I tried to get a glance while looking demure and intriguing. I then noticed that the boy she was ministering to was a boy who went to school with me. He was so cute, and he was always with the most popular girls. Just as I was fantasizing about him and his anticipated infatuation with me, Momma said, "Marelouise, (otherwise pronounced Mary Louise) get me some tape and a large bandage." Immediately, all the boys started laughing at the southern drawl pronunciation of my name, and I knew I had lost it all. Here was one more thing to be added to the list of things they constantly teased me about, such as my huge arm muscles and hairy legs. The next morning the scoutmaster took his troop back to the mainland so that the scout could receive real medical attention to his wound.

My sisters shared memories of their own dreams when the Coast Guard maneuvered the area during wartime, and they were stationed at Price's Inlet. They would tie up at our dock, and my sisters dressed in their finest shorts to flirt with the guys who stopped at the island for supplies. While neither married a Coast Guardsman, my sister Marcia did win the heart of a sailor she met at a church-sponsored service center downtown on Meeting Street.

During the long, hot summers, we had to make our own entertainment, and we played every game we knew and invented some of our own. During the day, we often swam or fished. Sometimes we made straw huts out of the dried sedge marsh and played "Queen of the Castle "or "Little Susie Homemaker." Other times, we chased each other around the bank of the pond, trying not to fall in as we jumped the washed-out areas. Other days we would make our favorite toy, a "roley-poley"to race down Little Beach. A roley-poley is simple to make. Many of our toys were homemade because we just did not have funds for store-bought toys. Poppa used to make us all wooden boats that we sailed and raced for fun as well.

DIRECTIONS FOR A ROLEY-POLEY

To make a roley-poley, take an empty gallon or quart paint bucket and hammer down the top gently, then drill a hole in each end. String a long piece of wire through the holes and secure the wire with a knot on the outside, with a long piece extending toward the hands (or you can add string for the handle). Remove the lid of the bucket and fill the bucket with sand; then hammer down the top really hard so it won't come off during a fast turn or a battle. Once the roley poley is complete, you race it as fast as you can run. Then you do battle with your playmates by crashing the roley-poley into each other to see whose is built the best and survives the challenge. This was one of the cheapest toys I ever owned, and one with which we had a great deal of fun.

ROLEY-POLEY"

Crash them, smash them
Race them with glee

> There's no other toy
> Like a roley-poley.

At night, we settled down to the radio, or a game of cards or Monopoly, using kerosene lights to illuminate the playing area. Poppa finally installed a generator that he would crank up on only special occasions. Still we begged many a time for the treat. *Gunsmoke* and *The Squeaking Door* were two of our favorite radio programs, and we never wanted to miss a night of the continuing sagas. Card games varied from poker to hearts, and a unique game called "smut." We played hearts with a slightly different twist: The person who got caught with the most hearts in their hand had to drink as many glasses of water as their points totaled. Perhaps that's one reason I drink over one hundred ounces of water each day. Smut was a dirty game. The player who got caught with the most cards left had a dab of smut put on his/her face for each point in his/her hand. The smut was retrieved from inside the burner lid off the wood stove. By the end of the night, your entire face was black. Whenever the boys played poker for matchsticks, I begged to play as well, but they were only obliging if they were short one player.

Poppa had several rifles he used for marsh-henning, and we loved to test our skill by setting bottles up in the marsh and shooting at them. Whoever lost would have to go into the marsh area among the glass, debris, and oyster shells to reset targets. Sometimes we tried shooting at the signs across the marsh. Most of us learned to handle a shotgun in some form or another in our preteen years. I never had the courage to shoot at a living bird, but I do love to shoot skeet or still targets in the marsh. Handline fishing was about the only form of fishing we knew. Rod-and-reel equipment was too expensive, and we only had an occasional taste of using it when one of the yachtsmen offered us a try.

A handline is made by rolling heavy cord on an empty stick of wood, then placing a hook and sinker on the end. These were used from the dock areas of Price's Inlet and Schooner Creek, as well as out in a bateau up one of the other side creeks. We used fiddlers to fish for sheepshead off the docks and at the sheepshead racks. The china-back fiddler is used for fishing because the fish won't bite on the black fiddlers. When they do bite, they leave the shelled back intact, and eat the soft part of the crab. Other than sheepshead, we caught small spot tail bass, whiting, blowfish and most of all the dreaded toadfish. Toadfish are the slimiest fish, with a wide mouth full of teeth; they always love to swallow the bait whole, making it necessary to cut the hook out of their mouths. I could not stand to touch a toadfish, and I would always sweet-talk Lilly into taking them off for me. She loved to fish as well, and we'd sit on the end of the dock talking, fishing, and dreaming. Lilly would tell us about her boyfriend who was coming to take her away one day. It seems that even Lilly, who lived in a world we did not fully understand, dreamed about her knight in shining armor who never came for her. My husband, Robert, loves to tease about capturing one of the "island girls," but we didn't meet on a fancy yacht. He moved to Charleston from Lake City his senior year of high school, and we dated off and on my junior year. We broke up my senior year, and got back together after I graduated. At the publishing of this book, we will have been married for almost fifty years.

Casting for fish and shrimp was popular with my brothers, and especially with Poppa. He could fan that net just like popping open an umbrella, and it never came out of the water empty. Poppa put his own weights on the nets and always repaired the snags himself. Cast nests were used to catch fish for bate for shark traps or to catch shrimp. My brothers all learned the skill of repairing cast nets and shrimp nets.

Swimming or walking on the beach was another favorite thing to do. In fact, we swam at the dock walking barefoot out on the oyster shells never giving a thought to the sharks and other creatures that swam right around us. My brothers would dive off the creosote piling supporting the dock, but my fear of heights kept me from attempting this feat. Because we stayed in the water for so many hours at a time, yachtsmen often accused us of being half fish. I did not know that mermaids did not really exist until I was a teenager. Often when we swam, we would flip a bateau over to make an echo chamber then dive under and give each other secret messages while the person left outside would have to guess what we were saying. It is amazing the games you can contrive when store-bought toys are not available. We did not have many store-bought toys on the island. We did not even have floats, but we used an old inner tube as a substitute.

We loved to go to the beach and would beg Poppa to take us in one of the bateaux using an outboard motor, most often an Evinrude or Johnson. If he didn't take us, we had to row ourselves there, because he did not trust us running the engines alone. This is why most of us developed the skill of rowing a boat. Walking the beach, we would look for sand dollars, bullets, pinwheels, pin cushions, or possibly a coconut thrown overboard by one of the cargo ships. We spent many hours collecting items from the beach, such as antique bottles. Andrew had a really large collection that Hugo carried back to the deep. The only time I remember Poppa really getting angry with me was over a bottle he found on the beach. He suspected that it was an antique, and he gave me the task of carrying it from the dock to the house with instructions to be extremely careful. I had not made five steps when I dropped the bottle and it broke. Poppa yelled at me, and I started crying immediately. I told him I was sorry, and much later he did the same.

Big conch shells were collected as well as large clamshells, which my brothers used for ash trays or painted shrimp boats on the inside. My brother Dan was especially talented at drawing and painting birds, but he never chose to develop his talent further than for personal enjoyment. Junior was also skilled at drawing shrimp boats, and my son Richie inherited the Magwood talent for drawing. He could have been a professional artist if he had stuck with it.

Searching the soft sand for evidence of turtle tracks, we ventured behind the sand dunes of the upper beach to look for a sea turtle nest. If we found a nest, a long probing iron was used to test the ground to see if there was actually a nest. If the eggs were hatched, we would dig up the nests to try to help the turtles make it to the sea. Baby turtles have a tremendously hard time surviving because the nests are often prey for the wild coons that rove the beaches and love to feast on turtle eggs. If a nest does survive through the hatching stage, then the baby turtles have to fight their way down to the sea trying to avoid the swooping sea gulls that eat them as a delicacy. Once, we happened upon a nest just at the moment hundreds of baby turtles were digging their way out and launching out for the sea. We gathered baby turtles and placed them into the sea, then ran back and forth from the nest to the beach trying to scare away the gulls before they could capture their prey. I took about four baby turtles back to the island with me and put them in our pond so I could watch them grow. When sea turtles are ready to die, they beach themselves something like a whale does. Through the years, we found many female turtles weighing around three hundred pounds or more decaying in the sands of Capers and Bulls Beach. Turtle eggs used to be eaten by many people in the early forties and fifties. When I was young, I ate hard-boiled turtle eggs, though I don't think I would do so now. When you boil a turtle egg, the white never gets hard. We hunted turtle eggs often until turtles were placed on the endangered species list, and protection methods, such as the turtle exclusion devices impelled on shrimp boats, were established.

When we were in the mood for island cuisine, we donned oyster boots and went into the marsh to pick periwinkles off the marsh grass. Periwinkles, which are small seashore snails, were boiled in water with a touch of salt and retrieved from the dainty shell with a straight needle. I heard a few years back that periwinkles had become the newest delicacy in New York. Too bad we didn't try selling those earlier, too. Conch is another dish that is eaten largely in areas such as Key West in conch stew, conch fritters, etc., but we roasted them in the oven. When the conch was done, the hard muscle would extend far out of the shell so you could pull the rest out easily with a fork. Behind the muscle is a soft center we termed the "cheese." We ate every bit except the shell foot covering the muscle part of the conch. To this day, no one believes that I ate any of these island specialties.

CONCH CHOWDER

Crack and cut grinder out of conch
Cut the top of conch off (hard shell foot)
Cut the white meat of conch into small pieces
Tenderize in pressure cooker or beat until tender
Brown 4–5 strips butts meat or bacon in a pan
Dice and add 1 onion
Dice 4–5 medium potatoes
1–2 stalks of celery (or 1 teaspoon celery salt)
Salt and pepper to taste
Dash or 2 of Tabasco
3–4 quarts of water
Cook all on medium heat until conch is tender

CLAM CHOWDER

Substitute clams for conch and grind in meat grinder.
Add 2 cans of tomatoes
(Andrew's version of Momma's recipe)

*The grinder is the tool used by the conch to crack oyster and clam shells, because it feeds on both of these mollusks.

THE SLEEPY INLET

"AT TWILIGHT"

The sun draws the curtain
Across the vast expanse of blue,
Folding multi-hues of purple
To anguished shades of gray.
As the cloak of darkness approaches
To mark the close of another day,
My heart is bathed in sadness
At the beauty others see,
And I long to find some comfort
In the presence of your company.

"THE RESTLESS SEA"

Mary Magwood Causey

Like glass, your surface mirrors the changes of your face,
One day calm and peaceful with gentle ripples of your grace.
And so we cast our ropes to ride softly the sheets of endless peace,
We are tucked upon your bosom with no signs of release.

But just as quickly, your mirrored image begins to change,
And we're tossed into a chasm of waves with endless range.
The bow begins to plunge in and out of your fearless grip
And we try our best to maneuver to avoid a fatal rip.

Water, Ooh so much water, the sea shows its angry side,
And as we grip the oars now, our fear we cannot hide.
For it is up to you to show us mercy, but there is no relief
As you open up your mouth and suck us in with unbelief.

Dancing in the shadows, we see phantoms of your past,
Those who trusted you for safety but here met their last.
What fate lies for us as you spit us back for more;
Are we destined to wrestle with you or make it to the shore?

For miles and miles, you take us to a far and different place,
And here we begin to notice a difference in your face.
Peaks of white are softened by the blush of emerald green
That make you much less threatening, a bit more serene.

Then just as quickly as you changed from friend to unwanted beast,
You surrender us with dignity to a sandbar just to the east.
So with tired minds and bodies we fight with you no more,
But wade into the shallow waters that mark your calmer shore.

CHANGED FOR LIFE

Of all the memories that linger of the island, one experience molded and changed the path of my life forever. It was a warm, windy summer afternoon, and Momma, Earl, and I had just sat down to eat supper. Poppa and my brother Bucky had gone to the mainland for supplies earlier that day, and they would not be returning until the next afternoon's high tide. My brother Earl was thirteen and skinny as a rail. I was eight with silky, straight, black hair and weighing not much more than sixty pounds. Momma was about 5'1", and at that time weighed around 145 pounds. When Earl finished his meal, Momma instructed him to go to the dock to check the bateaux and make sure everything was tied down securely, as the afternoon threatened a slight storm with strong winds. Momma and I were finishing up and preparing to clear the table when Earl came hurriedly through the house calling for Momma. He began to tell her how one of the bateaux had somehow broken loose from the mooring where my brother had set a shark line, and that he was going to put an outboard on another bateau and try to retrieve it. Momma instructed me to clean off the table and do the supper dishes while she went with Earl to try to retrieve the wayward boat.

I started clearing off the supper table on the screen porch where we always had our meals, singing as I always did to keep myself company. I boiled the water on the stove to prepare for washing the dishes, and while I was waiting on the water, I decided I would go to the dock and check to see if Momma and Earl were back. I walked the quarter-mile oyster shell path, glancing out to the inlet for any sign of the boat with Earl and Momma, but there was nothing at all in sight. Upon reaching the dock, I called loudly across the inlet, my voice echoing back in the emptiness. At that point, I did not worry too much, because I thought that possibly they had ventured up one of the side creeks and were just not visible from my vantage point. I walked back to the house, my dog Rex tagging along beside me.

The hot dishwater ready, I filled the pan, washed the supper dishes, and placed them in the drainboard for drying. Once the chore was complete, I decided to go back to the dock once more to see if Momma and Earl had returned. Again, I walked the path, searching for some sign of them in the inlet as I traveled. Hues of purple faded to anguished clouds of gray signifying the fast approach of dusk and the end of the day. Once I had reached the dock for the second time with still no one in sight, my trust and emotional calm turned to feelings of fear and doubt. I frantically called out for Earl and Momma, but there was no response and no boat anywhere in sight. My fear turned to panic, as I sat down burying my head between my hands and crying for God's help. My dog Rex, at my side, gently licked the tears from my cheeks, and I wrapped my arms around his neck seeking comfort anywhere I could find it. Knowing that darkness would soon surround me and being afraid of what might lay wait in the darkness, I walked hastily back to the house, frightened and helpless.

As I entered the back door through the living room, my eyes caught the picture of the Lord's Supper hanging on the wall over an old armchair. I felt drawn to that picture, and I found myself kneeling in the chair, eyes closed and head bowed. I sobbed uncontrollably as I sought the God to whom I had vaguely been introduced in an Episcopal Sunday School. I prayed innocently through tears as I pleaded, "Jesus, Jesus, please don't let my momma die! Please don't let my brother die!" Suddenly, an unusual calm came over me, and I heard a voice telling me everything would be okay. He would save my momma and my brother, and He would also save me. The voice instructed me to go to my momma's room and lie down and sleep. I walked to the bedroom, threw myself on the bed, and hugged the pillow as sobs rocked my body until finally I slept. As if from a dream, I awakened to hear the voice of my momma calling my name. I jumped from the bed, ran into the living room, where Momma grabbed me and hugged me tightly. Her clothes were soaking wet!

Momma led me to the kitchen where she began to boil water to make a "hot toddy," and she began to relay the story of what had happened. She and Earl had managed to reach the other bateau, and Momma had tied a rope from their boat to the oarlock of the wayward boat. Without notice, the wayward boat was swamped by a large wave and began to sink, pulling their boat down along with it before Momma could get the rope untied. Both boats sank, leaving Momma and Earl to fight the strong currents that swell below the surface as the waters rush back out into the Atlantic. There was one huge problem! Momma did not know how to swim; unusual for someone who had lived and worked around water all of her life. She said that she was not afraid of the sharks lurking beneath the deep or the water swelling around her mouth, pulling her quickly down. All she could think about was what might happen to me, an eight-year-old, alone on the island. Perhaps this thought kept her from panicking and losing sight of Earl, who had managed to grab hold of one of the oars. He swam to her and had her hold on to the oar as he swam and pulled her along. The swift currents had carried them almost three miles out into the Atlantic down Capers Beach close to Dewees Inlet. Earl fought the current and the elements until he was able to get near the shallow bottom of the beach. Once reaching the safety of the beach, he and Momma had to walk the three miles back around to our side of the inlet. Earl then left Momma on the back end of Capers while he swam back across to our island to get another bateau to come back and rescue her. They had to row back to the island soaked, frightened, and totally fatigued from the whole experience. When Momma got back to the house, the first thing she did was to make sure that I was okay.

Anyone who has lived through a miracle cannot question the event but must humbly bow to the authenticity of the One who has made it real. From that day forward, I knew without a shadow of a doubt that Jesus was the author of my miracle and my life. I vowed forever to give my allegiance to Him, following whatever path He chose for me. That year when we went back to school on the mainland, I asked if I could be baptized. Momma thought I was too young because many Baptists practiced the belief that the age of accountability was twelve, and I was only eight, too young, she thought, to truly understand my heart. After I talked with Rev. Lindler, he said, "Mrs. Magwood, she's ready," so I was promptly baptized so all would know the change that had come into my life. Jesus says that we must both believe in our hearts that God raised Him from the dead and confess with our mouths that He is Lord in order to be saved (Romans 10:9–10). Whatever is written in the instruction book of life, our Bible, is true. I know because He first chose me and allowed me to experience Him in truth for myself. At that point of my life, I did not truly understand sin, but as I grew in my faith, God opened my eyes to see the truth and caused me to understand the difference between right and wrong. If your life is somehow in shambles or you question the truth of God, please know that He is real. He desires to have everyone know and love His Son, Jesus, and to follow Him throughout life until one day He returns and takes us all to the next life, Heaven, with Him. John

3:16 tells us that "God so loved the world that He gave His one and only Son so that whomsoever believes in Him might be saved." It is really a simple process, know and understand God the creator, know and understand that we are all sinners, know that Jesus paid the price for our sin, and be willing to receive Him as Lord.

That traumatic and frightening day on the island set the course of my destiny to eternity as I made Jesus my personal savior. Since that time, I have tried to live my life for Jesus, seeking His will, yet falling short so many times. I am weak and born into sin. He died so that my faults and weaknesses would not keep me from having a relationship with God. It is through Jesus alone that we have life. But the uniqueness of that fact is that it is an abundant, passionate experience, a wave-ride we will never forget.

All through my childhood on the island, I talked with Jesus many a night from the dock underneath the stars. Sometimes, in the attic looking over the inlet or out to the marsh leading back to the city, I would sit at the window and discuss what He wanted in my life. I had a recurring dream until I no longer could decipher if it was real or not. I used to envision myself standing behind the chimney outside the old house, waving my arms in the air like a bird. I would do it fast and furiously until I could lift myself off the ground. After a while I not only lifted myself, but I could fly over people and imminent trouble that lurked beneath me. Although I have never had my dream professionally interpreted, I personally believe God has given me its meaning. It was His promise of always being there with me no matter what the circumstance or problem. On angel's wings He would lift me above the stress and strain, and through Him I would be able to overcome ("In Christ I can do all things." Phil 4:13). God never promised that we would not endure hardship as Christians, but that He would never put on us more than we could handle. Bearing things alone is a tremendous and unnecessary strain, but when God is on your side, there is nothing impossible because all things are possible with Him. After I found Jesus, my life on the island was more meaningful, because the loneliness was bearable, the beauty was more appreciated, and love for my family was multiplied. No one truly appreciates their childhood abode until they have grown up and can compare what they now have to what they once had. For some, memories are bitter and best forgotten, but with a loving family, they are priceless. Treasured memories are life's dreams fulfilled, so go forth and turn all your dreams into unforgettable memories.

THE SLEEPY INLET

Heroic Boy Saves Mother's Life As They Are Swept Into The Sea

By JACK LELAND
News and Courier Staff Writer

Add to the sagas of the sea the story of how 13-year old Earl Magwood helped save his mother's life when the two were swept out to sea after their boat sank near Bull's Island July 14.

The story didn't become known here until the Magwoods made their weekly trip to Mount Pleasant Thursday for supplies. Mr. and Mrs. Clarence Magwood and their children make their home on Little Bull's Island, between Capers and Bull's Islands.

Little Bull's Island, a three-acre cluster of cedars, lies on the western shore of Price's Inlet, one of the deepest and swiftest inlets along the coast. Just behind the east point of Caper's Island, the site is less than a mile from the open sea.

On July 14, Mr. Magwood went alone by boat to Mount Pleasant. With Mrs. Magwood on the island were Earl and his sister, Mary, 8. The mother-son ordeal of the sea began about 5 p. m.

Earlier that afternoon, Earl went down the inlet in a small outboard motor powered bateau to see to a "set" shark line which was attached to another bateau anchored near the inlet mouth. He found the bateau sunk and was unable to haul in its heavy anchor by himself because of the strong pull of a swiftly ebbing tide.

Earl went back to Little Bull's Island and enlisted his mother's help. They returned to the sunken bateau and attempted to hoist its anchor.

"We were pulling on the rope and I guess the tide just swept over our bow," Mrs. Magwood said. "It all happened in a second and the first thing I knew I was in the water with only an oar to hold onto."

The weight of the outboard motor sunk the bateau and the strong current swept them away from the anchored vessel.

Mrs. Magwood, who said she could manage to stay afloat but "couldn't really swim," gave credit to her son for keeping her afloat while a swift ebb tide swept them out of Price's Inlet and into the open sea.

"Earl grabbed me by one arm and I held on to the oar with the other and we drifted on out of the inlet," Mrs. Magwood said. "Several times I thought I was going down and I told Earl to leave me and save himself but he shook his head every time.

"I don't know how long it was but I suppose it was about an hour later that I felt sand beneath my feet and was able to stand up. We were on a shoal off Caper's Island but were separated from the island by a deep inlet about a mile wide."

After a short rest, Earl and his mother headed for shore. The youth swam, towing his mother who still clung to the oar. They reached the beach and walked eastward, back to Price's Inlet.

Schooner Creek, a deep tidal estuary, and a stretch of marsh remained between them and home.

"I told Earl I just couldn't make it cross Schooner Creek so he swam it alone and then bogged the rest of the way to our wharf," Mrs. Magwood said.

There he started an inboard launch and returned for his mother.

Asked if she was afraid of sharks while in the water, Mrs. Magwood replied, "Sharks didn't enter my mind. I was so worried about little Mary back on the island by herself that I didn't think about anything else. I knew she'd get awfully scared if we didn't come back."

And then she paid her son the greatest compliment a man can get.

"I'm really proud of Earl, he's a fine boy, my son," she said.

"YOU ARE NEARER THAN WE KNOW"

As I prayed today to you, Lord,
I felt a sadness deep within my soul.
I longed to feel Your presence,
To be filled until I once again was whole.
Your hand reached down and touched me;
My cheeks were wet with tears.
You tenderly brushed away each one
And calmed my inner fears.
You heard each prayer I offered
And I felt my spirit soar,
As I let You in much closer
Than You had ever been before.
Then I listened while You spoke to me
Of Things I still needed to do
To Rid My heart of worldly thoughts
So I could focus more on You.
You held me in Your arms awhile
Until I was strong enough to face the day.
You said, "Don't be afraid, my child,"
For I will never ever be far away.

"AT THE WINDOW"

I climb the brown plank stairs to the attic
Which holds the two windows of my world;
One across the waters of Prices Inlet,
The other the marsh creeks to the mainland.
Unlike mirrored images focusing inward,
The glass is transparent revealing objects
Altered only by the reflection of the sun.
Not once, twice, but three times I go
Seeking some small speck of hope to ease
The emptiness that bids me give way to misery.
At the mainland window, somehow, still I feel safe
Even as objects fade and disappointment lingers.
Across the water, the loneliness of the inlet
Mirrors the growing loneliness in my soul.
Alone, I yearn to converse with someone,
To share some laughter at a silly jest.
Majestically, the stars magnify heaven's expanse
And I feel God's presence billowing all around.
At the inlet window no fear, just joy and love
As tenderness bids me fill my empty soul.
We talk beyond the day's new dawn,
My body energized as if freshly charged,
And the empty inlet resting in perfect peace.

MARY MAGWOOD CAUSEY

FIRST LOVE"

Pound swiftly, heart, to match the sea,
And fill my head with your melody,
Like dainty sounding china bells
As feet meet tiny, pearly shells.

With gulls shrieking overhead
Until at last with fish they're fed
And wind whispering through the oats
Calling home the wayward boats,

As the waves crash upon the sand,
Erasing footprints of where we ran,
I, wrapped in the warmth of this place,
Close my eyes to feel your embrace.

"TEMPER"

Beneath the beauty bounds
A glimmer of dark light,
Like a rolling thunder cloud
On a starless summer night.

In the creeping shadows,
Lurks an ever-threatening foe
Awaiting the chance to surface
Like an arrow leaving the bow.

With voice tones raised an octave
Looks contorted and surreal,
One can witness a new creature
Affected by this strange ordeal.

For within us lie dormant
Feelings struggling to be free.
Yet anger is a matter of choice,
Learning to control it is the key.

"SOLITUDE AND SADNESS"

Far beyond the purple shadows at the parting of the day,
There lurks a powerful foe that will steal your breath away.
He enters in the solitude and silence buried deep within;
He forges the battle for your mind that he intends to win.

In the echoes of the waterfowl and wind caressing tide
Lurk imagined predators, and there's nowhere you can hide.
Fear grips you with a terror heightened by the setting sun,
And you want to find someplace that you can safely run.

But alone now with evil thoughts as your only company,
You find there is no other place that's safe for you to be.
So you drop your head and hide your tear-streaked face
Not wanting him to know he has brought you to this place.

And in your torment somewhere deep within
The scar begins to form that will surface again and again.
It will haunt you like a recurring dream with endless agony,
As you feel the sadness of this day and the almost tragedy.

Where is the power that can break the shadows of this past?
Where is the One who can give peace that will surely last?
Raise your head, oh little one, and dry your tears and rest,
For God has sent His angels to draw you safely to His breast.

He will not ever forsake you, nor let you feel alone,
But He will keep His hand upon you until all the fear is gone.
The darkness will not hurt you, or the shadows make you doubt,
That God is in the silence and solitude, and He's cast Satan out.

EPILOGUE

WHAT IS BEAUTY?

What is beauty? Man has tried to answer this question for thousands of years. The media would have us believe it is gorgeous men and women who have perfect bodies and faces. Others would say it is art or music. Still others see it as the wilderness untouched by human hands. Poppa saw it as the quiet, gentleness of Price's Inlet and the spirit he tried to protect from change.

Poppa used to tell me as a child, "Beauty is only skin deep, ugly is to the bone, beauty soon fades away, but old ugly holds its own." I had broken my front tooth in half at the age of eight while playing on my nephew's swing set. I was attempting a handstand on the round bars of the swing when the swing began to sway, knocking out half of my front tooth. After visiting our dentist, Dr. George Palmer, I was informed that the tooth would have to remain uncapped to ensure the nerve did not die, which he estimated to be around age fourteen. Living at Prices, this slight deformity did not make much of a difference because the worst kidding I received was from Earl and Tommie. I was already used to them teasing me about being adopted (with ten kids, what a joke!), so one more thing did not matter. At school, however, the story was totally different, because all the boys began calling me snaggletooth, a name that stuck with me through eighth grade. I graduated as salutatorian from grammar school and was allowed to begin taking high school classes in the eighth grade. I never smiled with my mouth open and was very shy. I believe this deformity kept me from making friends easily, but once I made a friend, that bond was not broken. I turned fourteen in October of my freshman year, shortly after school began, and I was finally allowed to have my tooth capped. That year, I was chosen from my ninth-grade homeroom to run for Miss Moultrie, our local high school beauty queen. Beyond my wildest expectations, and I am sure that of all of the other participants, I won the contest. The thrill of victory was reduced for me though, since neither Momma nor Poppa was there to see me win. In fact, they never saw me perform in any high school activity such as cheering, debating, or jumping rope for the PTA assembly. My brother Earl, however, was there and sat just behind the judges. He told me that he heard them saying, "There is just something about that girl that seems to radiate from within." I recalled what Poppa had told me through the years about beauty and realized that beauty is not something physical but spiritual.

For anyone who feels abused, rejected, dejected, or in some way unworthy, remember Poppa's saying; and from the words of our God who saw in David a mere shepherd boy, one with a heart like His. Beauty is defined by what comes from one's heart and not from what is on the outside. In fact, that is how Jesus sees each of us. He doesn't judge from the outside in but from the inside out. When Jesus lives on the inside of a person, His beauty radiates to the outside for all to see. It is the only beauty that endures unmarred by the sands of time.

Today, the island still sits diagonally across from Big Bulls and behind Capers Beach, although the houses are different because of Hugo. The dock still stands with the sign *Slow, No Wake*. My brother Andrew has taken on the family business of gathering oysters and clams. Because of the decline of the oyster production, however, clamming has become the bigger business. After Hugo, he rebuilt the little house on the island that belonged to Viola, where Junior and Alva once stayed, where Jimmy died, and that Andrew now calls home on his frequent stays. Andrew sold his shrimp boat and retired, so he can now spend many more days at the island. Family members enjoy going up for a weekend stay of fishing and reminiscing about life on the island with Momma and Poppa.

Many of my brothers and sisters, nieces and nephews, and some of my own children, still love to go to the island as a weekend retreat. The trip still requires a boat, but conveniences are much better than they once were. Electricity is available, and a telephone can be used for emergencies. A window unit provides air conditioning in the unbearably hot weather, and there is a refrigerator for easy storage of perishables. But the true charm of the island still exists: the warm, soft breezes blowing off the Atlantic, the sweet smell of the salt-water cedar and the marsh mud, the quietness away from humanity, machines, and noise. One can get away to calm the nerves and renew that quiet, inner-spirit that bids us to find peace. Many more people have learned of our island paradise, and almost every weekend the beaches and inlet are full of small boats out to enjoy a weekend getaway.

Once I had a vision of day trips to the island as a business. I envisioned my brothers' shrimp boats rigged for human passengers instead of shrimp, providing the thrill of the ocean by traveling the Atlantic passage through the narrow strait of the inlet to the dock. Once there, an oyster roast with trimmings in the winter and a Frogmore stew in summer would be a focal point of the trip. Side trips to the beach and fishing would give passengers individual choices, as well as a stop at the local shop featuring bird prints, shells with shrimp boats painted inside, dried seaweed, local shells, etc., all done by my family members. I realized, however, that paradise would no longer exist; commercialization would take over and money would become the target. Poppa never cared about the dollar, and the island should reflect the love for nature he had and the joy one finds in discovering a new life without the frills.

"WHAT IS BEAUTY?"

Her face is cracked and withered
Like toast that is stale and dry,
And her hair is thin and faded
Like a leafless tree at winter's nigh"

Her hands bear signs of labor
Like a man who digs outside,
While the veins in her legs protrude
Which no stockings will ever hide.

Judging by this exterior
No beauty would you see.
But the frame only holds the image,
True beauty lasts for all eternity.

Inside like sparkling wine,
A heart pure and true
Mirrors the smile of an angel
Who is genuine through and through.

So one then sees an awesome beauty
Not adorned by jewels or painted face,
But by a heart that is daily living out
The image of God's grace.

"MY HEART CRIES OUT IN ANGUISH"

My heart cries out in anguish
At the pain I cannot see,
The daily mental problems
Constantly plaguing me.

The debts I cannot settle,
The bills I cannot pay,
The things I cannot purchase
Only to live from day to day.

Why did I struggle upward
To be pushed so firmly down,
To build a stately mansion
And see it torn to the ground?

Would it not be better
To have less in life
Than to live each day
Combatting all this strife?

Or would the rise make a man
Of those seeking rich gain?
Is the battle invigorating enough
To forget about the pain?

My soul is single-minded
And the fight is not my own.
I give these problems to another,
The Greatest I've ever known.

In Him I shall find the comfort
That brings my mind to rest
And mends the scars of battle
That daily put me to the test.

Each day I shall be a victor,
Each day I shall start anew,
Remembering that God's my shield
And none can pierce me through.

SOME OF MY OWN FAVORITE RECIPES

SEAFOOD DELIGHT

1/2 lb. crab meat (or use 2 cans white claw meat)
1/2 lb. lobster or scallops
1lb. peeled and deveined shrimp
1 stick real butter
Salt and pepper
2–3 tablespoons Lea & Perrins white wine Worcestershire sauce
2 cups milk
1 cup shredded cheddar cheese
2 tablespoons flour
Dash of garlic (1/2–1 teaspoon as desired)
Melt butter in large saucepan and toss shrimp and scallops slightly
Add flour to brown
Add 1 cup of milk, salt, pepper, and white wine Worcestershire sauce
Add crab meat and second cup of milk

Mix thoroughly and add cheese
(May need a bit more milk if too thick)
Bake in casserole in oven at 350 degrees for about 30 minutes
Serve over penne pasta or linguini

SHRIMP FRIED RICE

1 diced onion (if desired)
2 tablespoons olive oil
4–5 cups cooked rice
1 lb. peeled and deveined shrimp
4–5 tablespoons light Kikkoman soy sauce
1 small box frozen baby green peas
Salt and white or black pepper to taste
Brown onion in olive oil and toss shrimp till done
Add rice and toss lightly, adding soy sauce along
Add box of green peas
Serve with fruit and salad
(Makes a great quick meal)

CAJUN STEAK

6–8 slices cube steak
Salt and pepper to taste
3 tablespoons flour
2 tablespoons paprika
2 tablespoons Cajun Creole seasoning
2 Tablespoons beef bouillon in 1 cup water
1 can no-fat beef broth
2 tablespoons olive oil
Mix flour with all seasonings
Coat steak well on both sides with flour and brown
in olive oil until done
Remove from pan and add 2 tablespoons
of flour mixture to remainder of drippings
Add beef stock and water, 1 can of beef broth
1–2 teaspoons Worcestershire sauce
Put meat back in pan on medium to low until gravy thickens
Eat over rice

TACO DIP

1 lb. ground beef
1 can of no-fat refried beans
1 small jar Pace picante sauce (med. or hot)
1 small tub sour cream
2 cups cheddar cheese
Taco seasoning mix
Brown beef, add taco seasoning
Add 1 cup water and cook on low about 30 minutes
Drain taco meat
Layer in casserole dish:
Refried beans, taco meat, picante sauce,
sour cream, and then cheese
Cook in oven at 350 degrees until cheese melts
Serve with taco chips

WHITE CHOCOLATE/MACADAMIA BARS

Melt 1 stick butter in a 9' x 13" pan
Add about 1 3/4 cups fine chocolate cookie crumbs
Chop 2 cups macadamia nuts and place on top of crumbs
Add 1 bag white chocolate chips
Add 1 small bag coconut
Cover with 1 small can of condensed milk
Bake in 350-degree oven until top is light brown

WHITE CHOCOLATE ALMOND BALLS

Melt 1 stick butter
Add 1 1/2 boxes of confectioners' sugar
2 teaspoons almond extract
1/3 cup Hershey's dark chocolate
1 cup chopped almonds
1 can of condensed milk
Roll into small balls and chill
Melt 1 bag white chocolate chips in 1 stick paraffin wax
Drop cold balls into hot mixture and cool on wax paper

COCONUT POUND CAKE

2 sticks Land-O-Lakes butter
1 1/2 pints whipping cream
3 cups flour
3 cups sugar
6 eggs
1 teaspoon vanilla
1 teaspoon lemon juice
7 oz. shredded coconut
Mix butter and sugar
Add eggs one at a time
Alternate whipping cream with flour
Add flavorings
Bake in 300-degree oven for about 1 1/2 hours in tube pan
or in 2 bread loaf pans

THE SLEEPY INLET

CHICKEN CHEESE POTATO SOUP

3–4 large potatoes
3–4 chicken breasts
6 bouillon cubes
1 box low sodium chicken broth
3 cups water
1 teaspoon s garlic salt
1/2 teaspoon celery salt
Salt and pepper to taste
1 teaspoon sweet basil
1 small jar Kaukauna cheddar cheese
½ cup instant mashed potatoes
½ cup heavy cream or milk

Cook chicken in broth and spices until tender, add potatoes in small chunks, and cook until tender. Add cheese and stir continually until dissolved. When completely blended, add about ½ cup instant mashed potatoes and ½ cup milk to thicken.

WHITE CHOCOLATE TOASTED COCONUT PIE

2 ready-to-bake pie shells (or make your own)
1 cup shredded coconut
2 cups heavy whipping cream
¼ Cup Splenda or sugar
1 cup milk
3 eggs beaten
1/2 bag white chocolate chips
1/2 cup shredded coconut toasted
1 teaspoon coconut extract
1/2 cup milk with 2 tablespoons corn starch

Mix Eggs with whip cream, flavoring, and sugar until blended. Cook on low heat and stir continually until dissolved. Add white chocolate, and stir until completely melted. Add coconut and continue to stir and blend in the cup of milk. Cook and stir occasionally until it begins to thicken then stir constantly. Add milk with corn starch mixture and cook until very thick. Pour into cooked pie shells.

HEALTHY CHICKEN BURGERS

10–12 ounces ground chicken breast
3–4 small portabella mushrooms
1/2 cup Asiago cheese
1 tablespoon Worcestershire sauce
2 teaspoons minced garlic
2 tablespoons sweet basil
1 teaspoon dry mustard
Sea salt and pepper to taste

Mix well and form into patties. Brown in pan sprayed with olive oil. Add about an ounce of chicken broth as they brown. Serve on whole grain English muffin with a slice of avocado.

SQUASH CASSEROLE

8 to 10 yellow squash or zucchini
1 cup herb stuffing
½ cup sour cream
1 small can cream of chicken soup
½ package Jimmy Dean hot sausage, cooked and drained
1 cup cheddar cheese
¼ teaspoon celery salt
1 teaspoon sweet basil
Salt and pepper to taste

Approximately 1 cup toasted onion topper
1 stick butter

Scrape squash and cut into small pieces then cook until tender. Drain squash and add all the other ingredients except onion topper and butter. When completely mixed top with onion topper and dot butter on the top. Bake at 350 for about 1 hour.

ACKNOWLEDGMENTS

A special thank-you to all of my brothers and sisters for their help with memories, recipes, illustrations, and pictures: in memory of Junior, Dan, and Earl who have all passed since this writing, and to Andrew, Marcia, Tommie, and Ann, the only ones who are left to share the joys of family. To my friend Barbara Smith, who always encouraged me to write, and to her husband, Henry, for help with pharmaceutical names—you're the best! Thanks especially to my friends, Donna Brown and Cindy Bohr, who read and reread and helped to edit the book. And to my husband who encouraged me to complete this work, I love you.

INDEX OF POEMS

"The Island"	vii
"Prisoner of the Sea"	x
"Shrimp Boats Are Coming In"	xi
"The Sandbar"	xii
"Junior-The Captain"	7
"Our Mother"	23
"Poppa's Peace"	25
"For Lilly"	26
"Gigging"	35
"Marsh-Hens"	36
"Catching Minnows"	37
"Fried Worms"	66
"Old-Time Remedies"	67
"The Plat-Eye"	71
Roley-Poley"	85
"At Twilight"	93
"The Restless Sea"	94
"You Are Nearer than We Know"	102
"At the Window"	103

First Love"   104
"Temper"   105
"Solitude and Sadness"   106
"What Is Beauty?"   111
"My Heart Cries Out in Anguish"   112

ABOUT THE AUTHOR

Mary Magwood Causey is a resident of Awendaw, South Carolina, where she lives with her husband, Robert. They have three children, Robert A. Causey Jr., Deborah Causey Yates, and Richard Anthony Causey (deceased), along with nine grandchildren. She is a graduate of the College of Charleston and a member of The Church at LifePark of Mount Pleasant.

Made in the USA
Columbia, SC
06 May 2018